The Founders' Facade:

Christianity, Democracy, Freemasonry, and the Founding of America

By

R. L. Worthy

KornerStone Books
6947 Coal Creek Pkwy
Suite 206
Newcastle, WA 98059

Published by

KornerStone Books
6947 Coal Creek Pkwy
Suite 206
Newcastle, WA 98059
Kornerstone@execs.com

Copyright ©2004 R. L. Worthy

All Rights Reserved. No part of this publication may be reproduced, stored in a retrieval system or transmitted in any form or by any means electronic, mechanical, photocopying, recording or otherwise, without the prior written permission of the publisher.

Design and Layout: KornerStone Books

Supervising Editor: Ethel Williams Thompson

Cover Photo: The Constitution of the United States
The Constitution is stored at the U.S. National Archives & Records Administration

Printed in the United States of America

The First Edition

ISBN: 0-9727627-2-8

In honor of those in every generation who've struggled for the Truth . . .

Prologue

The famous Roman Emperor Marcus Aurelius would teach: *"If it is not right do not do it; if it is not true do not say it."* Nobel Laureate Thomas Mann was to remark: *"A harmful truth is better than a useful lie."* And William Cullen Bryant would explain: *"Truth crushed to earth shall rise again . . ."* Each of these convictions rests in the understanding that although the arc of the moral universe is long—it bends toward justice! This is why Seneca could be so bold as to proclaim: *"Veritus Nunquam Perit"*: "Truth Never Dies."

Despite such timeless wisdom—we seem to live in a time in which millions cling to lies with no less fervor than a drowning man to a floatation device! However, the aggregate of a lie's believers does nothing to counteract its illegitimacy, or protect its followers from the ultimate consequence. Here I am reminded of the wisdom of Thucydides and Nietzsche: the former when he explained, the pronouncement that there is <u>safety in numbers</u> is the adage of the foolish—and the latter when he warns, <u>you do not want to be tricked by a liar because it is a misstep that could prove dangerous, injurious, and even fatal</u>!

Both of these observations are striking to me personally, considering that so many of my contemporaries are willing to embrace any falsehood that appears to afford them a slight advantage over someone else. Yet, if my life and research have revealed anything to me, they've established the following: nations can betray you; the wealthy can betray you; politicians can betray you; financial institutions can betray you; hell, a friend may even betray you—<u>but the truth cannot betray you</u>! As it was written long ago: *"Truth may be blamed but it cannot be shamed!"*

Today, it is agonizingly clear that perception and reality are two different things in America: the former seldom, in fact, jibing with the latter. For example, have you ever wondered why in a nation, which prides itself upon its Christian and Democratic principles—an honest leader is rare, and the numeric majority of poor and middle class citizens seldom prosper in real economic and educational terms? Or, why the numeric majority is practically never in a position to determine the course of the nation's most vital concerns? Perhaps, the answer is that the wealthy minority has done everything possible to ensure that the real majority never obtains a significant toehold!

Look, as a student of the history of the forefront, it goes without saying that there are a host of other subjects that I would rather be discussing with you. Yet, we have come to a time when nothing may prove more important than an understanding of this nation's foundations. Indeed, I believe this to be so crucial to your future that I have penned, The Founder's Façade: Christianity, Democracy, Freemasonry, and the Founding of America. In the words of Aristotle: *"He who thus considers things in their first growth and origin, whether a state or anything else, will obtain the clearest view of them . . ."*

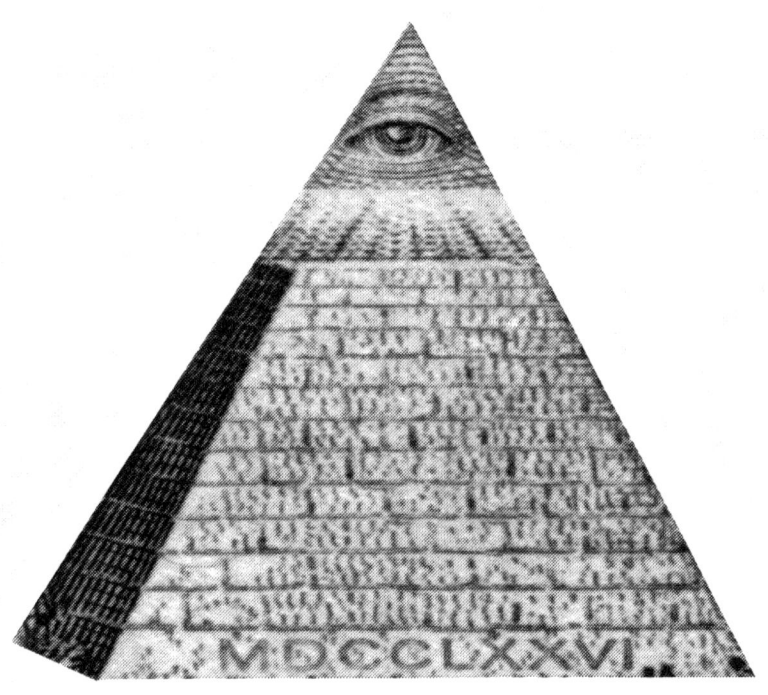

CONTENTS

Dedication	iii
Prologue	iv
Reader's Guide to the Work	viii
Map of the Original Thirteen States	viii
I. The Founders & Deism	1
The Early Colonists	2
Religious Freedom	7
The Deists versus the Christians	10
So Why all the Subterfuge?	19
Church & State	23
The Founders & Deism - Chapter Notes	25
II. The Founding Fathers & Democracy	26
The Republic	30
Façade	35
The Founding Fathers & Democracy - Chapter Notes	37
III. The FreeMasonic Foundations of these United States	39
Ancient Masonry	40
Medieval Masonry	42
Free-Masons	44
The Order of the Templars	45
Freemasonry & Spiritualism	47
The Great Coup d' Etat	50
Desaguliers & 18th Century Freemasonry	52
The Illuminati	54
Europe's Masonic Gulf	56
Freemasonry in Early America	57
America's Secret Society	60

CONTENTS

The American Craft's Unveiling	62
The Crusade Against Freemasonry	70
Albert Pike	77
The Plot to Seize America	82
Masonic Symbolism	84
Adams & Kennedy	92
The FreeMasonic Foundations of These United States - Chapter Notes	94

XVIII. Epilogue   96

Bibliography   98

Index   109

Order Form

Reader's Guide to the Work

Though trying to create a no frills straightforward document, I have been forced to employ the use of two time and space saving reference symbols: Roman numerals and the word net in parentheses (net).

A Roman numeral at the end of a sentence indicates reference cites and more information about the subject. The cite can be found in the corresponding chapter note located at the end of the chapter.

The word net in parentheses (net) at the end of a footnote has been used to indicate that the reference was found on the Internet. The precise url (website address) of the source is supplied in the bibliography.

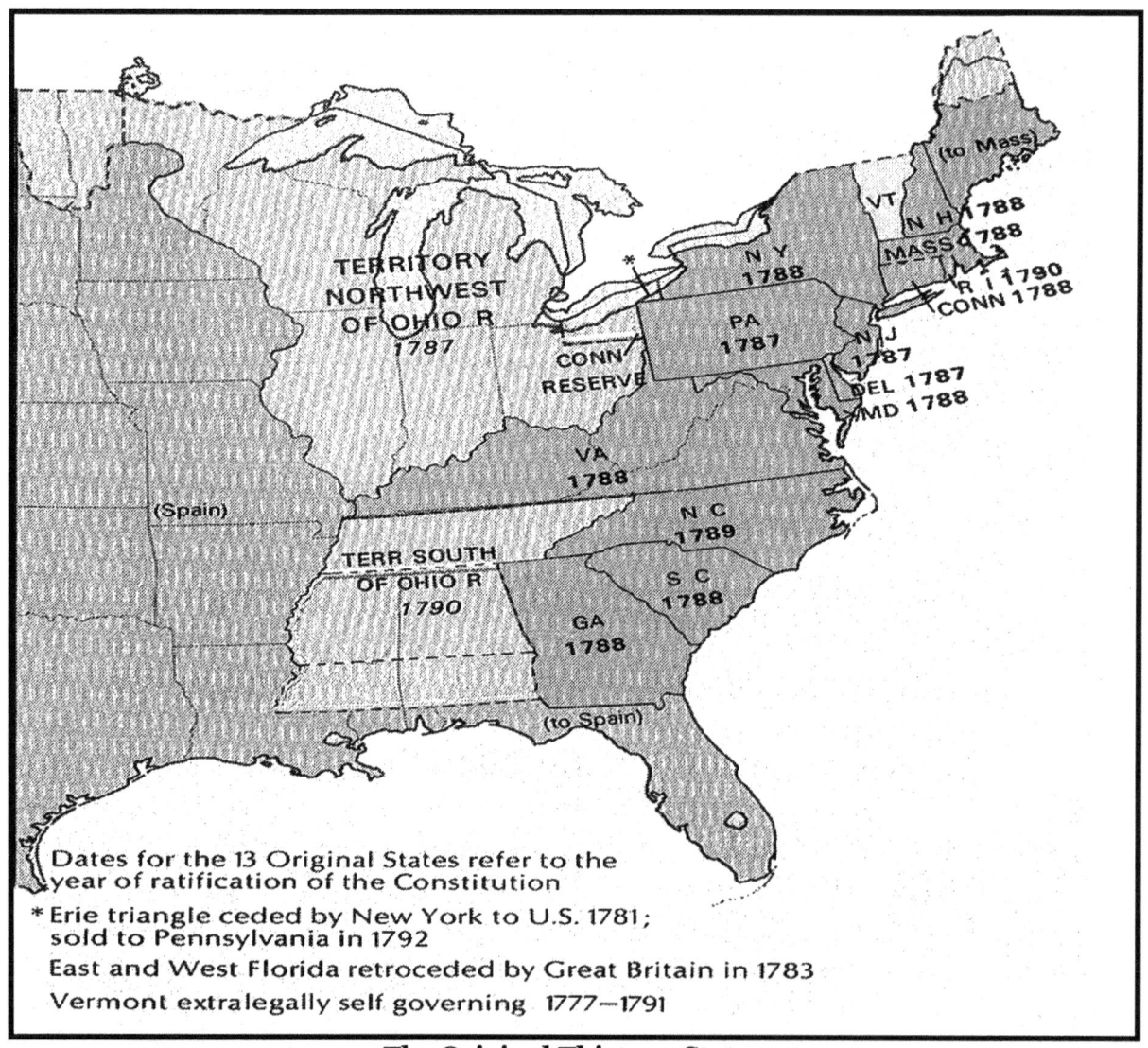

The Original Thirteen States

The Founders & Deism

The Founders & Deism

Aristotle wrote, *"He who thus considers things in their first growth and origin, whether a state or anything else, will obtain the clearest view of them."*[61] It has been advanced that the early settlers of the Thirteen Colonies were cut from England's finest spiritual and moral cloth: a people of an indubitable Christian character. Furthermore, the reason most often trumpeted for their crossing of the Atlantic Ocean was that these wonderful self-starters were people hell-bent in search of Christian freedom! However, neither of these notions wholly squares with the historical truth . . .

The Early Colonists

To begin with the first misconception, the establishment of a colony in the Americas was an undertaking with international ramifications. Accordingly, such a decision was hardly within the purview of the disenfranchised peoples of Europe. No, this was a step that could only be initiated by European royals and their wealthiest subjects! And this, without doubt, was the situation during the founding of England's colonies in North America. You see, having witnessed the wealth obtained by the Spanish through the colonization of the Caribbean and Central and South America, the rush was on between the remaining Western European countries to gain a footing in the New World. During the 17th century, wealthy Englishmen, Frenchmen, Swedes, and Dutch would all fight to secure territory in North America.

The Dutch captured Sweden's trading forts along the Delaware River in 1655: effectively ending the Swede presence. In turn, the British took the New Netherland Colony from the Dutch in 1664 and renamed it New York. That left the French and the English to vie for control of the Atlantic Sea coast. After decades of sporadic fighting, the French would

---

[61] Ropes, L., <u>Aristotle</u> p. 248

eventually withdraw from the Atlantic in 1673. Hence, the primary motivation for the crown to sanction warfare, and for England's merchant class to finance the first Atlantic expeditions was hardly spiritual, but entirely commercial! In deference to Caffrey:

> *"Under English law, all colonial territory belonged to the Crown. The easiest way for the monarch to administer it was to grant it by charter to companies or proprietors, who would then be responsible for future development . . ."*[62]

Another national benefit that was derived from sponsoring the colonizing effort was a reduction in the pressure placed on England's cities by their poor, uneducated, orphaned, and criminal element. In a paper entitled, <u>A Particular Discourse concerning Western Discoveries</u> the clergyman and geographer Richard Hakluyt of Bristol, contracted by Secretary Walsingham to develop colonial policy, did not only call for the need to secure the resources of North America from the French and Spanish—he would also submit that the colonization of North America could be a way to reduce England's criminal population by setting up merchants who had previously gone bankrupt and were serving time in debtor prisons. Atop this, he saw colonization as the perfect solution to England's growing vagrant population.

A copy of Hakluyt's paper was sent to the Queen Elizabeth; further, it just so happens that he had already been an acquaintance of Sir Walter Raleigh. Notestein would consider Hakluyt's paper a *"classic statement for English colonization."*[63] Even though Hakluyt's plan would

---

[62] Colony, <u>Universal Standard Encyclopedia</u> Vol. V, p. 1856 & Colonial Life in America, <u>The World Book Encyclopedia</u> Vol. III, p. 1586 & Colonial System, <u>The American Peoples Encyclopedia</u> Vol. V, p. 860 & Caffrey, K., <u>The Mayflower</u> p. 45 & Wallace, P., <u>The White Roots of Peace</u> pp. 50 - 61
The French and Dutch undertook despicable measures against the Iroquois nation to secure control the region's resources. However, with France's defeat at the hands of the British, the French would shift their attention to the Great Lakes and Mississippi River regions.
[63] Notestein, W., <u>The English People on the Eve of Colonization 1603 - 1630</u> pp. 255 - 256 & <u>The American Peoples Encyclopedia</u> Vol. XVI, p. 493, Vol. XIX, p. 677 & Caffrey, K., <u>The Mayflower</u> p. 14
Sir Walter Raleigh would lead England's first colonizing effort in North America. Though founded in 1585, for various reasons, the Virginia coast settlement would not gain any true stability before 1606.

The Founders & Deism

gain wide acceptance amongst England's upper crust, there were many who disagreed with it. For instance, Francis Bacon would remark that such a policy was akin to *"planting fields of thistles."*[64]

Moving from theory to practice, the Colony of Georgia, founded by wealthy Englishmen James Oglethorpe during the reign of George II, was perhaps the clearest example of the establishment of a colony from a prison population in North America. Not only did the release of the English prisoners alleviate a prison expense—it was also hoped that the Georgian colony would create a buffer against Spain's forces to the south in Florida! Additionally here, we find that Hakluyt's program was undertaken against England's orphan children. In a colonial newspaper of 1627 entitled, <u>1,500 kidnapped children imported</u> we read:

> *"More than 1,500 children who were kidnapped from the streets of London arrived in Virginia this year, many seek to work as servants. This practice has its origins in a policy adopted by King James I. In 1619, James decided that orphans had a better chance of finding a home and employment in the colonies . . . Criminals saw an opportunity to exploit the situation and have stolen children throughout London."*[65]

---

[64] Caffrey, K., <u>The Mayflower</u> p. 45 & Jeal, T., <u>Livingstone</u> pp. 2, 188 - 189, 222 - 223, 374 Frankly, Hakluyt's ideas were still popular a century later. In the 19th century letters of David Livingstone, the young explorer called for the lands of Africa to be colonized for two basic reasons. First, to take valuable crops and natural resources back to England for commercial gain. And second, the colonies would serve as an endless dumping ground for England's poor and uneducated, which would relieve urban pressures in England. In the words of Livingstone, *"If large numbers of the British urban poor emigrated to Africa they could begin new lives, no longer 'crowded together in cities . . . in close ill-ventilated narrow lanes.'"* Eventually, Livingstone would modify his view of British migration; i.e., only enough Whites should be sent to maintain influence and control over the lands and people of Africa. As decent in some respects as he may have come to be—the Anglophilia of the young Livingstone is unmistakable.

[65] Oglethorpe, James Edward, <u>The Encyclopedia Britannica</u> Vol. VIII, p. 886 & Oglethorpe, James Edward, <u>The American Peoples Encyclopedia</u> Vol. XIV, p. 981 & Oglethorpe, James Edward, <u>The World Book Encyclopedia</u> Vol. III, p. 1584, Vol. XII, p. 5857 & <u>Chronicle of America</u> p. 56 & Tatch, J., <u>Freemasonry in the Thirteen Colonies</u> pp. 73 - 74
James I is the same ruler who has been lauded for his version of Christian scripture—the King James Bible.

The Founders' Facade

In all fairness, the English were not the only country to send their undesirables abroad. A news article of 1721 entitled, French send prostitutes to New Orleans states:

> *"The shortage of women for colonists to marry has been relieved this year with the arrival of a group of females taken from a house of correction in France. Some of them are prostitutes. Others are orphans who were kept in the Salpetriere in France. When the ship carrying the females arrived at Ship Island near Biloxi earlier this year, women-hungry men paddled to the island in pirogues to greet them. Some of the women were married by a secular pries in Biloxi shortly after their arrival. The remaining women were parceled out to French settlements such as New Orleans, Mobile and Biloxi. The Company of the Indies, the John Law concern that was formerly known as the Company of the West, has continued to bring prostitutes, murderers, thieves and other undesirables to the Louisiana colony despite protests from Governor Bienville . . . Although Bienville has complained about the sending of convicts to the colony, he has repeatedly asked for wives for his colonists, particularly the Canadian soldiers here. In one of his letters, he pleaded, 'Send me wives for my Canadians. They are running in the woods after Indian girls.'"*[66]

The Pilgrims

Though a clear exaggeration to portray all of the colonists as having been criminals and orphans—you can see that it is no less fictitious to depict them all as pious Pilgrims. In truth, the Mayflower did not set sail for North America until 1620: decades after the colonizing effort had begun. Further, of the 102 Pilgrims who were to reach Plymouth Rock, 50 soon died and it was all the remaining 52 could do, to eke out a simple and meager

---

[66] Chronicle of America p. 94 & Caffrey, K., The Mayflower p. 45
In passing, the British would take a strikingly similar approach with the establishment of their Australian and Rhodesian colonies.

existence. Historians explain that had it not been for the humanity and moral dispositions of such Native Americans as Samoset, Chief Massasoit, and Squanto—<u>the Pilgrims would not have survived their first year</u>. Incredibly, despite despicable treatment by White settlers during his early life, including kidnapping and slavery—Squanto would teach the Pilgrims how to survive: (1) he taught them where to catch fish; (2) he taught them where and what to plant; (3) he taught them when to fertilize their corn; and (4), he guided them on many hunting and exploratory expeditions.[67]

As amazing as the account of the unchartered Plymouth Colony may be—<u>at no time should we consider the Pilgrims to represent the majority of the settlers of the British colonists</u>. By 1630, the number of Pilgrim immigrants may have been as high as 362; however, scholars estimate the total number of colonists at that period around 2500. By 1639 that figure would jump to 5700 settlers. And by 1649 that number would leap to some 27,900 colonists.[68] The statistics shared, the Pilgrims weren't merely in the numeric minority—they were a religious minority in the colonies as well. In fact, the reason why the Pilgrims did not originally join on with the already established Virginia Colony was for the well-founded belief that these loyalists of the Church of England would persecute them![69] For this reason,

---

[67] Caffrey, K., <u>The Mayflower</u> pp. 130 - 141 & Smith, B., <u>Bradford of Plymouth</u> pp. 148 - 152, 156 - 157
The number of early Pilgrim survivors varies from 52 - 54. Remarkably, Squanto would live with, and help, the Pilgrims for the remainder of his life.
[68] Carruth, G., <u>The Encyclopedia of American Facts and Dates</u> pp. 6 - 10, 16
In 1691, the Plymouth Colony would merge with the Massachusetts Bay Colony.
[69] Caffrey, K., <u>The Mayflower</u> pp. 28, 41, 46, 131, 177, 181 - 182, 280 - 281 & Smith, B., <u>Bradford of Plymouth</u> pp. 20 - 21, 154, 222 & Pilgrim, <u>The World Book Encyclopedia</u> Vol. XIII, p. 6336 & Augarde, T., <u>The Oxford Dictionary of Modern Quotations</u> p. 80 & Kohn, G., <u>Encyclopedia of American Scandal</u> p. 2 & Seldes, G., <u>The Great Quotations</u> p. 193
The term <u>Pilgrim</u> was chosen to denote a traveler to, or seeker of, a holy place. George Santayana would later say: *"The true Christian is in all countries a pilgrim and a stranger."* Here are a few of the customs and beliefs of the Pilgrims: Sabbath began Saturday evening at 6pm; their Sabbath sermons could be given by many members; organs were not permitted in their churches; kneeling in church was prohibited as it was seen as a Catholic practice; marriage was a civil, rather than religious, agreement; Christmas and other holidays were not celebrated; grace was said before and after meals; games of chance and gambling were sinful; witchcraft was punishable by death; Pilgrims were forbidden to work for non-Pilgrim colonists; and the original colony was founded upon a communal (communist) model, however, that would later be altered so that crop harvests did not <u>have to be shared</u> equally.

The Founders' Facade

and several other irreconcilable differences with the early European settlers, the Pilgrim Governor William Bradford would be compelled to make a strong moral distinction between his people and the majority of the European colonists, stating—*"We are Saints"* and they are *"strangers."*[70] No single remark better highlights the difference between people who seek the spiritual path—and those content to practice a religion . . .

Religious Freedom

Truth be told, the Pilgrims were not the only religious minority to be persecuted by the European settlers of the North American colonies. The 17th century Parliament and Church of England, under Oliver Cromwell, would become highly Puritanical (Calvinist) Protestant. Hence, from the middle 1600s in England, anyone whose religion was different was labeled a Nonconformist.[71] But, of course, this sentiment did not cease with the transatlantic crossing of the English settlers. According to Hoffer:

> *"Equal protection of the laws did not forbid special privileges—quite the contrary; gender, wealth, family, political position, and, above all, religious persuasion made*

Parenthetically, that a fervently religious people should create a communist colony is no surprise to a historian. For example, centuries before the founding of the Plymouth Colony, Clement would say: *"The use of all things that are found in this world ought to be common to all men. Only the most manifest iniquity makes one say to the other, 'This belongs to me, that to you.' Hence the origin of contention among men."*

[70] Pilgrims, The, The American Peoples Encyclopedia Vol. XV, p. 777 & Smith, B., Bradford of Plymouth p. 191, 198, 222 & II Corinthians 6: 14 - 18

The Christian sentiment of separation from worldly governments and their aims was not an invention of the Pilgrims. Indeed, the Apostle Paul taught: *"Do not harness yourselves in an uneven team with unbelievers. Virtue is no companion for crime. Light and darkness have nothing in common. Christ is not the ally of Beliar, nor has a believer anything to share with an unbeliever. The temple of God has no common ground with idols, and that is what we are—the temple of the living God. We have God's word for it: 'I will make my home among them and live with them; I will be their God and they shall be my people. Then come away from them and keep aloof, says the Lord. Touch nothing that is unclean, and I will welcome you and be your father, and you shall be my sons and daughters, says the Almighty Lord.'"*

[71] Nonconformist, Oxford English Dictionary Vol. X, p. 489

a difference in one's legal status. The Puritan way of worship in congregational churches and Puritan religious doctrine, a stern version of Calvinism, were established by law in Massachusetts and Connecticut, and woe be to the Quaker or other sectarian who persistently flouted the will or questioned the privileges of these favored institutions . . ."[72]

In reality, those colonists who faced religious persecution in England faced the same prejudice in North America. What's more, those settlers who dared to defy the mandates of the Church of England in the colonies could be subjected to the harshest of penalties! Many reports survive which discuss religious persecution in the North American colonies:

- A Boston article of 1651 entitled, <u>Baptists arrested; one publicly whipped</u> explains:
"Dr. John Clarke and Obediah Holmes, two members of the Baptist sect, which this city's religious leaders consider a prejudiced and ignorant one, were arrested in Lynn this month for holding an unauthorized religious meeting. The two Baptists, who reject infant baptism and the standing order of the colony, were holding a service in someone's home when the sheriff arrested them. Clarke, a friend and colleague of Roger Williams in Rhode Island, which proper Bostonians regard as a sewer of filth, was imprisoned. But the Baptist minister from Newport was later freed without punishment. Holmes was whipped in the streets of Boston. The Governor, John Endecott hopes that such punishment will serve to deter encroachment from the neighboring colony by people he finds schismatic and disruptive."

- A decade later we find <u>Quakers hanged for resisting banishment</u>:
"Two men of the Quaker sect, which Boston's authorities regard as pestilential and disruptive, were hanged today on Boston Common. William Robinson and Marmaduke Stevenson, along with Mary Dyer, were led from their cells under a 200-man guard . . . The three have been repeatedly transported from the colony, the last time under penalty of death should they return. However, they showed their disregard for the city fathers by returning again. The authorities, carrying out their previous threat, sent the Quakers to the gallows. Following the executions of Robinson and Stevenson, Dyer was led to the gallows. She was blindfolded and the noose was placed around her neck. Before the

---

[72] Hoffer, P., <u>Law and People in Colonial America</u> p. 18 & Rogers, J.A., <u>Sex and Race</u> Vol. III, p. 12

sentence could be carried out, however, her son interceded on her behalf. As a result, she is once again to be transported out of the colony, never, the authorities hope, to return. The bodies of her two compatriots were thrown into a pit as an example to any who might consider religious dissent."

- Also, a 1660 article entitled, <u>Quaker is hanged for re-entering colony</u> reports:
"Mary Dyer, after sorely and repeatedly trying the patience of the Commonwealth of Massachusetts, was hanged today. Dyer, who escaped the noose last year through her son's intervention, once again violated the directive of the authorities by re-entering the colony to spread the doctrines of Quakerism. What the authorities regarded as rebellious disobedience forced her hand in the end. She showed neither remorse nor contrition when she spoke after her sentencing . . ."[73]

While executions were not an everyday occurrence, as the upper crust (gentry) of the early settlements were exactingly loyal to the Church of England—the common notion that the colonies were a place where every man was free to worship as they pleased is nothing more than that—<u>a notion</u>. As a matter of fact, by the early 18th century the Church of England was exercising a great deal of authority over the lives of the colonists. For example, colonial inhabitants were required to pay a church tax—the largest part, of course, being slated for the Church of England. In Virginia it was illegal to challenge any Bible scripture. In Georgia, South Carolina, North Carolina, New Jersey, and New Hampshire—colonists had to practice the Protestant religion; and in Pennsylvania, colonists had to either attend church on Sunday or prove that they had a proper private worship service in their homes. Oh' yes, and but of course—just the mere accusation that someone practiced witchcraft was grounds for torture and the death penalty.[74]

---

[73] <u>Chronicle of America</u> p. 66, 68, 71
[74] Barker, C., <u>American Convictions: Cycles of Public Thought 1600 - 1850</u> p. 7 & <u>Chronicle of America</u> p. 82 & Witchcraft, <u>The American Peoples Encyclopedia</u> Vol. XX, p. 191 & (Video), History's Mysteries: <u>Witchcraft</u> History Channel
The colonists took their lead, no doubt, from the peoples of Europe. Between the 14th and 16th century in Europe (principally Germany and France) anywhere from 60,000 to 300,000 men, women, and children were killed after being accused of practicing witchcraft.

The Deists versus the Christians

Moving on into the second century of colonial life, we come to the time of the founding of the thirteen original United States. Irrespective of the modern custom of declaring the founders devout Christians who should be held just a little lower than the angels, once again, the hyperbole fails to square with historical fact! Actually, the most cursory examination provides us with undeniable proof that these men were neither Christians nor deserving of any comparisons to the Christian God's angels. Quite frankly, the spiritual philosophy that would hold greatest sway over the founders was Deism. Researchers maintain:

> "**Deism**, *the belief in a personal transcendent God Who created the world but does not intervene in its affairs. According to this doctrine, the world operates and develops eternally on the basis of mechanical and unchanging laws established by God. Rejecting the belief in revelation from God, Deism holds that, by the light of reason and an understanding of nature, the individual may determine for himself religious doctrine and practice . . . In accordance with the prevailing philosophy of rationalism, they sought to establish Natural Religion, based on reason and experience, in place of institutionalized religion, based on faith.*"[75]

In laymen's terms, while believing in the concept of a creator, Deists do not adhere to a particular religious doctrine or creed; i.e., Judaism, Christianity, Buddhism, etc. Furthermore, Deists do not believe that the creator interjects Himself into the daily affairs of

---

[75] Fresia, J., Toward an American Revolution pp. 3 - 4 & Universal Standard Encyclopedia Vol. VII, p. 2289, Vol. X, p. 3456 & Gay, P., Voltaire: Philosophical Dictionary Vol. II, p. 479 & Deism, Encyclopedia of Religion Vol. IV p. 262 & Robertson, J., Short History of Freethought p. 3 & Kelly, C., Conspiracy Against God and Man p. 46
Robertson writes, *"Before 'Deism' came into English vogue, the names for unbelief, even deistic, were 'infidelity' and 'atheism.'"* Other appellations for 18th century Deists were Theists and Freethinkers.

individual humans. Also, at the core of the doctrine was the idea that understanding Nature in this dimension would lead to the comprehension of the Deity. In accordance with this philosophy, we find <u>The Unanimous Declaration of the Thirteen United States of America</u> making no mention of Jesus Christ or Christianity—but expressly containing the phrases: *"the laws of nature"*; *"of nature's God"*; and *"divine Providence."*[76]

Despite the fact that there is little mention of Deism in America's scholastic history books today—the philosophy was openly embraced by many of the leading minds of 17th and 18th century Europe. For instance, Robertson explains that John Locke's aversion to Christianity would eventually force him outside the parameters of genteel British and Irish society. Both, Counte Constantin Volney and Charles de Secondat Montesquieu wrote critically of Europe's religious institutions. In fact, the latter would remark: *"Under moderate governments, men are more attached to morals and less to religion; in despotic countries, they are more attached to religion and less to mortals."*[77] The French philosopher Jean Rousseau would

---

[76] Walters, K., <u>Rational Infidels: The American Deists</u> pp. 38 - 39 & Demott, B., <u>Freemasonry in American Culture and Society</u> p. 6 & <u>The Unanimous Declaration of the Thirteen United States of America</u> & Walters, K., <u>The American Deist: Voices of Reason and Dissent in the Early Republic</u> p. 74 & Locke, John, <u>Encyclopedia of Philosophy</u> Vol. IV, p. 499, 502 & Locke, J., <u>The American Peoples Encyclopedia</u> Vol. XII, pp. 633 - 634 & <u>Chronicle of America</u> p. 197 & <u>The World Book Encyclopedia</u> Vol. II, p. 778, Vol. X, p. 4552 & Seldes, G., <u>The Great Quotations</u> p. 461, 568 & Johnson, R., <u>Religious Right Lie: America is a Christian Nation</u> The World Union of Deist (net)

In passing, the wording in the aforementioned, and the <u>Bill of Rights</u>, demonstrates the clear influence of Locke's <u>Treatises on Government</u> over Jefferson and Hamilton. Living almost a century earlier, John Locke was an English physician who had been employed and backed by the adversaries of the Stuart kings, to publicly denounce their desire to obtain absolute power. Locke would essentially say that there is no such thing as a king's natural authority, but that every citizen has a right to life, liberty, and property. Hence, in his view, the only purpose for government was to protect the rights of individuals—anything more was an over extension or intrusion. Here is a sample of Locke's commentary—it may call to mind the Declaration of Independence: *"The necessity of pursuing true happiness (is) the foundation of our liberty."* And as well, *"The state of nature has a law of nature to govern it, which obliges everyone; and reason, which is that law, teaches all mankind who will but consult it, that, being all equal and independent, no one ought to harm another in life, health, liberty or possessions."*

[77] Hall, M., <u>The Secret Teachings of All Ages</u> p. XIX & Robertson, J., <u>Short History of Freethought</u> p. 308 & Walters, K., <u>The American Deist: Voices of Reason and Dissent in the Early Republic</u> pp. 182 - 184 & Locke, John, <u>Encyclopedia of Philosophy</u> Vol. IV, pp. 501 - 502, Vol. V, p. 371

The Founders & Deism

make it widely known that he could not accept the belief that the incarnation of the Christian Christ could atone for human sin. Indeed, he would declare: *"Whoever dares to say: 'Outside the Church is no salvation,' ought to be driven from the State."*[78] Conversely, the celebrated French intellectual Francois Voltaire would proclaim the following about Deism:

> *"The great name Deist, which is not sufficiently revered, is the only name one ought take. The only gospel one ought read is the great book of Nature . . . The only religion that ought to be professed . . ."*[79]

Before long, the philosophy of Deism was spreading across Western Europe. Frankly, at one point, French Deists were replacing the Christian symbols on their churches with depictions of Rousseau and Voltaire! The Deistic movement in Britain would be led by such notable figures as Lord Herbert of Cherbury, Thomas Hobbes, Charles Blount, David Hume, John Toland, Antony Collins, Thomas Chubb, Thomas Morgan, Henry Marten, and Matthew Tindal. The two leading Italian Deists were Giordano Bruno and Lucilio Vanini. The most noted Deist of Holland was Barukh Spinoza. Finally, in Germany Hermann Reimarus, Gotthold Lessing, and Immanuel Kant were Deism's greatest champions.

Historians explain that intellectuals of the European nations were not the only people to embrace Deism.[80] If the truth is to be told, the somewhat modest intellectual class that was to be found in the colonies considered Europe to be the source of culture and learning; hence, the ideas of men like Rousseau and Voltaire are known to have had a profound influence upon the beliefs of the founders. Case in point, allow me to share these words of the prolific Thomas Paine:

---

[78] Seldes, G., The Great Quotations pp. 164 - 165
[79] Rousseau, Jean, Encyclopedia of Philosophy Vol. VII, p. 223 & Woods, R., The World Treasury of Religious Quotations p. 225 & Seldes, G., The Great Quotations p. 61
[80] Hall, M., The Secret Teachings of All Ages p. XIX & Cavendish, M., Man, Myth & Magic Vol. IV, p. 562 & Deism, Encyclopedia of Philosophy Vol. II, pp. 327 - 333 & Deism, Encyclopedia of Religion Vol. IV pp. 262 - 263 & Robertson, J., Short History of Freethought pp. 297 - 299, 310 - 323 & The Encyclopedia Britannica Vol. II p. 580, Vol. XI, pp. 99 - 100 & Vanini, Lucilio, Encyclopedia of Philosophy Vol. VIII, pp. 232 - 233

The Founders' Facade

"There are times when men have serious thoughts, and it is at such times, when they begin to think, that they begin to doubt the truth of the Christian Religion; and well they may, for it is too full of conjecture, inconsistency, improbability and irrationality, to afford consolation to the thoughtful man. His reason revolts against his creed. He sees none of its articles are proved, or can be proved . . . Here it is that the religion of Deism is superior to the Christian religion. It is free from all those invented and torturing articles that shock our reason or injure our humanity, and with which the Christian religion abounds. Its creed is pure, and sublimely simple. It believes in God, and there it rests . . . it avoids all presumptuous beliefs, and rejects, as fabulous inventions of men, all books pretending to revelation."[81]

In reality, many colonists were aware of the fact that patriots the likes of Ethan Allen, Ben Franklin, George Washington, Thomas Jefferson, James Madison, James Monroe, and Thomas Paine were not Christians—but stalwart Deists! In 1794, a fervent Deist by the name of Elihu Palmer would form the Deistical Society of America in New York. The organization's first order of business was to muster support for the French Revolution, and to establish a *"republican religion"* known as the *"cult of the Supreme Being."*[82]

It is hardly surprising to find Christian leaders of the period, on both sides of the Atlantic, set squarely against the Deistic movement. As early as 1564, the staunch Calvinist Pierre Viret would bitterly attack Deists for rejecting the Bible and the divinity of the Christian Christ! In a discussion of atheists in his Anatomy of Melancholy—Burton explained that although many of Europe's philosophers and Deists were moral men—they nevertheless

---

[81] Paine, T., Of the Religion of Deism Compared with the Christian Religion The World Union of Deist (net) & Seldes, G., The Great Quotations p. 60
This was a brief excerpt of Paine's denunciation of Christianity and the Bible. Yet, to his credit, Paine would also remark: *"Infidelity does not consist in believing or disbelieving; it consists in professing to believe what one does not believe."*
[82] Deism, Encyclopedia of Philosophy Vol. II, p. 334 & Seldes, G., The Great Quotations pp. 257 - 258 & Johnson, R., Religious Right Lie: America is a Christian Nation The World Union of Deist (net) & Robertson, J., Short History of Freethought p. 376 & Chronicle of America p. 212 & Walters, K., Rational Infidels: The American Deists pp. 192 - 230

were little more than atheists.[83] Eventually, the Church would ban with the royals to try to find ways to stop Deism. For example, people who openly practiced Deism in England could be subjected to fines, lose their civil rights, and even sentenced to life in prison.

Although separated by an ocean, we find the concern of America's clergy over the spread of Deism to have been no less grave. The Rhode Island Congregationalist David McClure was to assert: *"(T)hough their talents may be brilliant, their motives are despicable and dangerous."*[84] In 1820, William Blake would say to the world:

> *"You, O Deists, profess yourselves the Enemies of Christianity, and you are so; you are also the Enemies of the Human Race and of Universal Nature . . . Deism, is the Worship of the God of this world by means of what you call Natural Religion and Natural Philosophy, and of Natural Morality or Self-Righteousness, the Selfish Virtues of the Natural Heart."*[85]

For the Record

In view of all the agenda-driven religious propaganda that's hurled at us today, indulge me as I commit the offence of sharing the actual words and religious practices of several of the most heralded and influential figures of the early nation. This is crucial to your understanding because not only does their behavior force us to conclude that the founders were Deists—but that they possessed an aversion for Christianity:

- Allow me to begin with a few remarks by Thomas Jefferson:
"*Millions of innocent men, women, and children, since the introduction of Christianity, have been burnt, tortured, fined, imprisoned; yet we have not*

---

[83] Deism, Encyclopedia of Philosophy Vol. II, p. 327 & Robertson, J., Short History of Freethought pp. 300 - 304
Burton's document was written in 1621.
[84] Deism, Encyclopedia of Religion Vol. IV p. 263 & Schwartz, B., George Washington: The Making of an American Symbol p. 172
[85] Woods, R., The World Treasury of Religious Quotations p. 225

The Founders' Facade

advanced an inch towards uniformity. What has been the effect of coercion? To make one half of the world fools, and the other half hypocrites. To support roguery and error all over the earth."

He would also state, *"It does me no injury for my neighbor to say there are twenty gods, or no God."* Here is Jefferson's position on the Christian trinity:

"No one sees with greater pleasure than myself the progress of reason in its advances towards rational Christianity. When we shall have done away the incomprehensible jargon of the Trinitarian arithmetic, that three are one, and one are three . . ."

In his <u>Syllabus of an Estimate of the Doctrines of Jesus, Compared with Those of Others</u>, Jefferson says: *"I am a good Christian, a man who reveres Jesus, though I cannot accept his godhood."* Finally, of the Christian Church Thomas Jefferson remarked:

"No man complains of his neighbor for ill management of his affairs, for an error in sowing his land, or marrying his daughter, for consuming his substance in taverns . . . in all these he has liberty; but if he does not frequent the church, or then conform in ceremonies, there is immediate uproar."

- James Madison, who is commonly considered to be the "Father of the Constitution" would write in his <u>Memorial and Remonstrance against Religious Assessments</u>:

    "During almost fifteen centuries has the legal establishment of Christianity been on trial. What have been its fruits? More or less in all places, pride and indolence in the Clergy, ignorance and servility in the laity; in both, superstition, bigotry and persecution."

- The famed military commander and author Ethan Allen would declare:

    "I have generally been denominated a Deist, the reality of which I never disputed, being conscious I am no Christian, except mere infant baptism makes me one; and as to being a Deist, I know not strictly speaking, whether I am one or not."

- Alexander Hamilton is purported to have been opposed to the presence, and/or prayers, of Christian clergy at the nation's first Constitutional Convention. The reason most commonly given is that Hamilton feared *"some disagreeable animadversions"* rising from the participation of Christ's representatives.

- Turning to writings of Thomas Paine we find:

    "The study of theology, as it stands in Christian churches, is the study of nothing; it is founded on nothing; it rests on no principles; it proceeds by no authorities; it has no data; it can demonstrate nothing; and it admits of no conclusion. Not any thing can be studied as a science, without our being in possession of the principles upon which it is founded; and as this is not the case with Christian theology, it is therefore the study of nothing."

    He would further remark: *"All national institutions of churches, whether Jewish, Christian or Turkish, appear to me no other than human inventions, set up to terrify and*

The Founders & Deism

enslave mankind, and monopolize power and profit." We also find him saying: *"One good schoolmaster is of more use than a hundred priests!"* And finally:
"I do not believe in the creed professed by the Jewish church, by the Roman church, by the Greek church, by the Protestant church, nor by any church that I know of. My own mind is my own church."

- While George Washington would not be so bold in word as his contemporaries—his actions, nevertheless, make it impossible for objective observers to misread his spiritual disposition. Actually, in his many writings and speeches—George Washington never claimed to be a Christian or that his Lord was Jesus Christ. According to Boller:
"Broadly speaking, of course, Washington can be classified as a Deist . . . The Supreme Being whose aid he counted upon Washington usually called Providence, Heaven, or, to a lesser extent, God . . . he also made much use of such stock Deist phrases as Grand Architect, Governor of the Universe, Higher Cause, Great Ruler of Events, Supreme Architect of the Universe, Author of the Universe, Great Creator, Director of Human Events, and Supreme Ruler."

To their credit, both Davis and Boller have stepped forward to explain that stories of George Washington's prayer vigils at Valley Forge are nothing but sheer fabrication. Frankly, the Valley Forge tale was widely known to have been the concoction of the Anglican Minister Mason Weems. This minister would also dream up the tale of the young George chopping down a cherry tree, and not being able to tell a lie about doing it. Not content there, incredibly, Weems would even go so far as to make analogies between Washington and Moses of the ancient Hebrews. However, many Christians of the period were unable to share in Weem's aggrandizement of Washington. As a matter of fact, many Christian leaders were not merely aware of, but openly disturbed by, the sitting President's Deism! In Boller's <u>George Washington and Religion</u> we find:
"In a sermon delivered in October, 1831, which attracted wide attention when it was reported in the 'Albany Daily Advisor,' [Episcopal Minister Bird] Wilson stated flatly that 'among all our [six] presidents from Washington downward, not one was a professor of religion, at least not of more than Unitarianism [the exceptions being John and John Q. Adams].' Washington, he went on to say, was 'a great and good man, but he was not a professor of religion'; he was really a typical eighteenth-century Deist, not a Christian . . . Wilson also declared that Dr. James Abercrombie, assistant rector of Christ Church in Philadelphia, which Washington attended while President, had confided to him, that Washington never partook of the sacrament of the Lord's Supper . . . On sacrament days, Wilson quoted Abercrombie as saying, 'Washington's custom was to rise, just before the ceremony commenced, and to walk out of church!"

Wilson was not alone in his assessment: the Philadelphia clergymen Bishop White, Frances Wright, Robert Owen, and David McClure would all attempt to bring the truth to the public. Of course, each later generation has produced and supported its own versions of Weems, to ensure that the messianic shadow of the "Father of the Country" should never fade. This notwithstanding, allow me to share one last finding about Washington as I believe nothing could speak to his spiritual disposition more: *"Even on his deathbed Washington asked for no ritual, uttered no prayer to Christ, and expressed no wish to be attended by His representatives . . ."*

- Permit me to conclude with the celebrated Ben Franklin, as the case is easily made that no man would have a greater influence upon the thinking of the founding fathers of America than he! Unlike Washington, the man whose likeness appears on the nation's one hundred dollar bill, was hardly cryptic or apologetic, about his Deism. Thus, I need not cite such Franklin maxims as, *"lighthouses are more helpful than churches,"* or *"The way to see Faith is to shut the eye of Reason,"* to bring his outlook upon spirituality to light! Rather, I would simply like to share this brief excerpt of a letter from Benjamin Franklin to Ezra Stiles:

"You desired to know something of my Religion . . . Here is my Creed. I believe in one God, Creator of the Universe. That he governs by his Providence. That he ought to be worshipped. That the most acceptable Service we can render him is doing good to his other Children. That the soul of man is immortal, and will be treated with justice in another Life respecting its Conduct in this . . . As to Jesus of Nazareth, my opinion of whom you particularly desire, I think the system of morals and his religion, as he left them to us, the best the world ever saw or is likely to see; but I apprehend it has received various corrupting changes, and I have, with most of the present dissenters in England, some doubt as to his divinity . . ."[86]

---

[86] Seldes, G., The Great Quotations p. 149, 150, 160, 161, 163, 167, 257, 422, 775, 806, 944 & Johnson, R., Religious Right Lie: America is a Christian Nation The World Union of Deist (net) & Barker, C., American Convictions: Cycles of Public Thought 1600 - 1850 p. 264 & Brodie, F., Thomas Jefferson: An Intimate History p. 25, 371 & Koch, A., Philosophy of Thomas Jefferson p. 26 & Peterson, M., Thomas Jefferson & The New Nation: A Biography & Madison, James, The World Book Encyclopedia Vol. XI, p. 4692 & Madison, James, American Peoples Encyclopedia Vol. XII, pp. 926 - 927 & Morris, R., Seven Who Shaped Our Destiny p. 226 & Jones, R., George Washington & Walters, K., Rational Infidels: The American Deists pp. 8, 38 - 39, 44 & Walters, K., The American Deists: Voices of Reason and Dissent in the Early Republic pp. 209 - 213 & Boller, P., George Washington and Religion pp. 8 - 11, 14 - 18, 93 - 94 & Robertson, J., Short History of Freethought pp. 378, 380 - 381 & (Video), Booknotes: Kenneth Davis Interview: Don't Know Much About History C-Span 9/91 & Jay, T., Encyclopedia of Fads and Fallacies pp. 177 - 178 & De Gregorio, W., Complete Book of U.S. Presidents p. 22, 93, 107 & Peabody, J., The Founding Fathers: John Adams A Biography in His own Words pp. 32 - 35 & Lafeber, W., John Quincy Adams and the American Continental Empire & Unitarian, The World Book Encyclopedia Vol. XVII, p. 8284 & Unitarianism, The America Peoples Encyclopedia Vol. XIX, p. 260 & Schwartz, B., George Washington: The Making of an American Symbol pp. 2, 171 - 172, 174 - 176 & Chronicle of America p. 107, 269 & Writings: Franklin p. 1179 & Buxbaum, M., Critical

The Founders & Deism

Nothing more really need be said, insomuch as the Christian scripture explains—"<u>*He who denies the Son, denies the Father.*</u>"[87] However, I will add this one caveat, in that true followers of the way understand that a tree is known by its fruit. In light of the fact that these Deists have been canonized for coining such phrases as, *"Don't Tread on Me," "Taxation without Representation,"* and *"We hold these truths to be self-evident, that all men are created equal"*—but would then sanction the wholesale deception, vile treatment, and murder of the Native American for his land—and become very wealthy from the uncompensated labor and brutalization of millions of kidnapped Africans—<u>wrapping it all in the guise of carrying out their "Christian" mandate</u>—is it any wonder that Thomas Jefferson should remark: *"Indeed I tremble for my country when I reflect on God's justice, that it is just, and it will not sleep forever . . ."*[88]

<u>Essays on Benjamin Franklin</u> pp. 4 - 5, 7, 147 - 167 & <u>Famous Masons</u> (net) & <u>List of Famous Freemasons</u> (net) & Schlesinger, A., <u>The Age of Jackson</u> pp. 350 - 360
Johnson explained that Jefferson was to advise his nephew, Peter Carr, to approach the Bible in the same way that he would the writings of Livy or Tacitus. The 3rd President would also succeed in having professorships in classical languages like Hebrew and the theological area of study dropped at William and Mary College—with departments of contemporary languages, medicine, and law replacing them. Brodie would observe of Jefferson: *"He despised clergymen all his adult life ."* As a stalwart Deist, Washington felt no need to submit to, or supplicate in honor of, the Christian Christ. In the words of Schwartz: *"George Washington's belief and practice of Christianity was limited and superficial, because he was not himself a Christian. In the enlightened tradition of his day, he was a devout deist-just as many of the clergymen who knew him suspected."* According to Bird Wilson, the Presidents George Washington, Thomas Jefferson, James Madison, and John Monroe were Deists. John Adams and John Quincy Adams were Unitarians. Yet, as Unitarians reject the divinity of the Christ, they too, cannot be deemed Christians. I have little cause to doubt Wilson's assessment in regard to Andrew Jackson who was a high-ranking Freemason; but in all fairness, some label Jackson a very lax Presbyterian.
[87] I John 2:23
[88] Jones, R., <u>George Washington</u> pp. 78 - 79 & Fresia, J., <u>Toward an American Revolution</u> pp. 1 - 2, 14 - 20 & <u>Chronicle of America</u> p. 107 & Platt, S., <u>Respectfully Quoted</u> p. 202
"We hold these truths to be self-evident, that all men are created equal, that they are endowed by their Creator with certain unalienable Rights, that among these are Life, Liberty and the pursuit of Happiness." Rather incredible declaration considering the following: George Washington would have as many as 216 slaves; Jefferson would have as many as 185 slaves; James Madison would enslave as many as 116 Blacks; George Mason of Virginia would have as many as 300 slaves; William Blount of North Carolina was a slaveholder; Pierce Butler of South Carolina was a slaveholder; Oliver Ellsworth of Connecticut certainly was not opposed to the institution; Franklin would not oppose slavery on moral grounds, but economic profitability; William Samuel of Connecticut was indifferent to the plight of slaves; Luther Martin was of Maryland was a slaveholder; John Mercer of Maryland was a slaveholder; Charles Pickney and Charles C. Pickney of South Carolina were slaveholders;

The Founders' Facade

So Why all the Subterfuge?

As for the subterfuge around Christianity and the founding fathers, the reason is extremely simple—they were a relatively learned group that wanted to create a country of trusting and passive followers. Historically speaking, religion has proven an important tool in that endeavor. Hence, the founders would take a much more utilitarian, rather than spiritual, course when it came to the matter of religion and formation of the new nation. Accordingly, the founders would heed the teaching of the classical writers of Europe regarding the role of religion in the state. Allow me to share a few examples of that instruction with you here:

- Greece's Polybius would observe:
  "Since the masses of the people are inconsistent, full of unruly desires, passionate, and reckless of consequence, they must be filled with fears to keep them in order. The ancients did well, therefore, to invent gods, and the belief in punishment after death."[89]

- Diodorus Siculus taught, *"The myths about Hades and gods, though they are pure invention, help to make men virtuous."*[90]

- Rome's Seneca stated, *"Religion is regarded by the common people as true, by the wise as false, and by rulers as useful."*[91]

- Aristotle wrote:
  "A tyrant must put on the appearance of uncommon devotion to religion. Subjects are less apprehensive of illegal treatment from a ruler who they consider godfearing. On the other hand, they do less easily move against him, believing that he has the gods on his side."[92]

- Indeed, several centuries later, we even find the heralded Ibn Khaldun of the Moors

---

Edmund Randolph of Virginia would have as many as 200 slaves; and, John Rutledge of South Carolina was a slaveholder.

[89] Seldes, G., The Great Quotations p. 430
[90] Murphy, E., Diodorus on Egypt p. 4
[91] Seldes, G., The Great Quotations p. 827
[92] Seldes, G., The Great Quotations p. 936

The Founders & Deism

stating:

"Vast and powerful empires are founded on religion. This is because dominion can only be secured by victory, and victory goes to the side which shows most solidarity and unity of purpose. Now, men's hearts are united and coordinated, with help of God, by participation in a common religion . . . Religious fervor can efface the competitiveness and envy felt by the members of the group towards each other . . . nothing can stand in their way, for their outlook is the same and the object they desire is common to all and is one for which they are prepared to die . . ."[93]

What's more, as devotees of the philosophical views of Rousseau and Locke, the founders were well acquainted with the pronouncement: *"Since no man has a natural authority over his fellow, and force creates no right, we must conclude that conventions form the basis of all legitimate authority among men."* Also, as it pertains to the Christian religion in particular:

"I am mistaken in speaking of a Christian republic; the terms are mutually exclusive. Christianity preaches only servitude and dependence. Its spirit is so favorable to tyranny that it always profits by such a regime. True Christians are made to be slaves, and they know it and do not much mind: this life counts to little in their eyes."[94]

---

[93] Fletcher, R., Moorish Spain p. 106 & Huart, C., A History of Arabic Literature p. 352
[94] Walters, K., Rational Infidels: The American Deists pp. 12 - 21 & Seldes, G., The Great Quotations p. 154, 230 & Eigen, L., & Siegel, J., The Macmillan Dictionary of Political Quotations p. 616 & Inside the Third Reich: Memoir by Albert Speer p. 96 & Kick, R., (ed.), YOU ARE BEING LIED TO: The Disinformation Guide to Media, Historical Whitewashes and Cultural Myths p. 294

These remarks were made by the heralded Rousseau. In truth, utilitarian opposition to the faith was still being expressed in Europe centuries later. In the words of Hitler: *"You see, it's been our misfortune to have the wrong religion. Why didn't we have the religion of the Japanese, who regard sacrifice for the Father land as the highest good? The Mohammedan religion too would have been much more compatible to us than Christianity. Why did it have to be Christianity with its meekness and flabbiness?"* To be fair, such sentiment is still bandied about by America's upper crust: please permit Ted Turner's characterization of Christianity as *"a religion for losers"* to suffice here. Look, how could it be any clearer—serving God and His Truth—and merely being used to obtain worldly aims are two completely different matters! Yet, in the face of the expression of such secular and utilitarian attitudes towards Christianity—one cannot help but be struck by the fact that two millenniums ago the North African theologian Tertullian would declare: *"Nothing is more foreign to us Christians than politics . . ."*

The Founders' Facade

Such teachings and philosophical outlooks shared, are we really to be surprised that the heralded Ben Franklin should write: *"Wise Governments have always thought religion necessary for the well ordering and well being of society . . ."*[95] Or, even more, that the Deistic Washington should concur and integrate religion into the handling of his troops? Actually, despite being lauded for ordering his soldiers to attend chaplain led church services on Sundays—Washington's expressed rationale for the order was the favor of *"Heaven,"* hopes that the services would reinforce *"regularity and decorum,"* and stem *"profane cursing"* and *"drunkenness."* The blessings of heaven, decorum, and to curb drunkenness—hmmm: as for the first, that could mean anything forasmuch as Diabolis himself has dwelled in heaven; as for the second, Christ was often criticized for tending to be informal in his dealings with others; and third, many of you are aware that the Messiah himself has been referred to as a *"glutton"* and a *"winebibber."* In truth, the principal mission of the Christian Christ was to bring salvation through grace to mankind—an objective that George Washington couldn't have given a care about.[96]

In all honesty, historians are hard-pressed to refute the observation of the France's de Tocqueville that America's early leaders considered the tenets of the Christian religion *"necessary to the maintenance of republican institutions."*[97] In deference to Schwartz, in his George Washington: The Making of an American Symbol we find:

> *"Following a tradition transmitted from Cicero through Machiavelli, to their own contemporaries . . . the less pious men of the time saw in religion a necessary and assured support of civil society. <u>Although guided by their own secular traditions,</u>*

---

[95] Writings: Franklin p. 149

[96] Boller, P., George Washington and Religion pp. 52 - 53 & Revelations 12: 9 - 11 & Matthew 11: 19 & (Video), The Riddle of the Dead Sea Scrolls 1990 & Qumran, Grolier Multimedia Encyclopedia & Pesher, Encyclopaedia Judaica Vol. XIII, p. 331 & Douglass, J., New 20th-Century Encyclopedia of Religious Knowledge p. 628 & Pfeifer, C., The Dead Sea Scrolls and the Bible

[97] Walters, K., Rational Infidels: The American Deists p. 3 & Tocqueville, Alexis, World Book Encyclopedia Vol. XIX, p. 308

de Tocqueville was a noted French aristocrat and historian who visited and traveled throughout the United States between for two years (1831 - 1832). After his travels, de Tocqueville wrote Democracy in America.

The Founders & Deism

they felt that only religion could unite the masses and induce their submission to custom and law. The belief was formed amongst these men that, the Gospel is our greatest safeguard, for it governs in secret as well as in public . . ."[98]

Coming to grips with this utilitarian view of Christianity does not merely account for the tremendous duplicity of the so-called upper deistic crust of the early nation—it also explains all of the subterfuge one encounters when questions about their devotion to the teachings of Christ arise! As one noted historian was to put it:

"Sympathizers with deistic rationalism hesitated to go public because of their fear that dissemination of the new way of thinking would undermine social stability. Many colonial intellectuals attracted to deism were also suspicious and contemptuous of what they tended to think of as the 'mob.' They feared that a diminution of the normative and ecclesial authority of traditional Christianity would open the floodgates of anarchy. The 'common' people, in their estimation, were too boorish and too unlettered to appreciate or profit from a religion founded upon reason and nature, and therefore needed artificial and institutionalized standards to control their behavior. The deists thought it better to allow the mob to retain its faith in conventional Christian beliefs until such time as it was better educated and hence more receptive to the dictates of rational conscience. Until that day arrived, deism was best confined to the genteel drawing room and the gentleman-scholar's study."[99]

---

[98] Schwartz, B., George Washington: The Making of an American Symbol p. 173
[99] Walters, K., Rational Infidels: The American Deists pp. 6, 8 - 9 & Seldes, G., The Great Quotations p. 305 & Fresia, J., Toward an American Revolution p. 5 & The Writings of Henry D. Thoreau: Frequently Asked Questions (net)
Diogenes (The Cynic) said, *"The foundation of every state is the education of its youth."* That said, the Walters continues: "American colleges were the first settings to be infected by public infidelity . . . Yale, for example, had earned a somewhat exaggerated reputation for free though [Deism] Lyman Beecher, who became a student there in 1793, later recalled that the college was (then) in a most ungodly state . . . The college church was almost extinct . . . Most of the class before me were infidels, and called each other Voltaire, Rousseau, D'Alembert . . .' Nor was Yale the exception. Apostasy raged at any number of other institutions of higher learning. Virginia's College of William and Mary was known as a training ground for 'infidelity.' In 1799, the College of New Jersey (Princeton) had 'only

Church & State

Finally, let me state that these men's indignation for the mixing of Christianity and daily government was never far from the surface of their politics. For example, James Madison, the Father of the Constitution, would declare: *"Religion and government will both exist in greater purity the less they are mixed together."*[1] Paine exclaimed, *"The adulterous connection of church and state."* And Jefferson would not merely characterize the combination of church and state as *"loathsome,"* he would also say:

> *"History I believe furnishes no example of a priest-ridden people maintaining a free civil government. This marks the lowest grade of ignorance, of which political as well as religious leaders will always avail themselves for their own purpose."*[2]

In actual point of fact, the Virginia statute that's so often celebrated for ensuring religious freedom—might just as well be said to have been the statute that established freedom from religion for the founders of the new nation. Authored by Jefferson, and pushed through the legislature by Madison, the statute is worded thus:

> *"<u>No man shall be compelled to frequent or support any religious worship, place, or ministry whatsoever</u> . . . the rights hereby asserted are of the natural rights of

---

three or four (students) who made any pretensions to piety. A 1789 alumnus of Dartmouth College recalled 'but a single member of the class of 1799 was publicly known as a professing Christian.' Even Harvard became enmeshed in free thought . . ." In his <u>The Mode of Education Proper in a Republic</u>, Benjamin Rush wrote: *"I consider it possible to convert men into republican machines. This must be done, if we expect them to perform their parts properly in the great machine of the government of the state."* I cannot help sharing that while Emerson was to declare Harvard University a teacher of most of the branches of learning— Thoreau's reply would be: *"Yes, indeed, all of the branches and none of the roots!"*

[1] Eigen, L., & Siegel, J., <u>The Macmillan Dictionary of Political Quotations</u> p. 613
[2] Seldes, G., <u>The Great Quotations</u> pp. 167 - 168

mankind, and that if any act shall be hereafter passed to repeal the present or to narrow its operations, such act will be an infringement of natural right."[3]

Once more, this is hardly a ringing endorsement of Judeo-Christian worship by the founding fathers. While the apologists will claim that Jefferson's wording was chosen in response to the stern mandates that were imposed upon the colonists by the Church of England—not only had the revolution been fought and won—the fact is that these words speak for themselves: "<u>No man shall be compelled to frequent or support any religious worship, place, or ministry whatsoever.</u>" In that he has captured the actual sentiments of the founders so well, permit me to share this comment by Walters:

> *"The American deists were opposed uncompromisingly, to supernaturalist religions in general and Christianity in particular. They insisted, for example, that the latter's central tenets—revelation, miracles, eternal damnation, the depravity of human reason, the divine authorship of Scripture, the divinity of Jesus and the triune nature of Godhead—are unworthy of the Deity's dignity and an assault upon the rationality of humans . . ."*[4]

Thus, despite all the rhetoric, there is no doubt that the central figures of the founding of the United States, as well as its early presidents, did not believe in Christianity. This is even attested to by the nation's currency. Irregardless of the words *"In God We Trust,"* and possessing esoteric and spiritual symbols—the words <u>Jesus</u> and <u>Christ</u> are nowhere to be found—nor are the likes of such traditional imagery as the shepherd, cross, or fish. So that you won't ever be misled again, allow me to close with this remark by Thomas Jefferson:

> *"It is not to be understood that I am with him (Jesus Christ) in all his doctrines. I am a Materialist; he takes the side of Spiritualist."*[1]

---

[3] Barker, C., <u>American Convictions: Cycles of Public Thought 1600 - 1850</u> pp. 264 - 265
Though Jefferson's wording in the Virginia statute is absent from the Constitution's 1st Amendment—his sentiment is clear as a bell: "<u>Congress shall make no law respecting an establishment of religion</u>, *or prohibiting the free practice thereof . . .*"
[4] Walters, K., <u>Rational Infidels: The American Deists</u> p. 39

The Founders & Deism - Chapter Notes

[i] Seldes, G., <u>The Great Quotations</u> p. 150, 524 & Robertson, J., <u>Short History of Freethought</u> p. 382 & Pledge to the Flag, <u>The World Book Encyclopedia</u> Vol. XIII, p. 6419 & Ron's Currency, Stocks & Bonds: <u>History of U.S. Paper Money</u> (net) & <u>Lawmakers blast Pledge ruling</u> CNN.Com/Lawcenter (net)

It is to be noted that the currents of Deism in American politics did not come to a sudden end with the death of the founders. Indeed, no less a figure than Abraham Lincoln would state: *"My earlier views on the unsoundness of the Christian scheme of salvation and the human origin of the scriptures, have become clearer and stronger with advancing years and I see no reason for thinking I shall ever change them."* President Grant was said to possess a similar view of religion. If the truth is to be told, none of the figures whose likenesses appear on the nation's paper currency professed to be Christian: Washington—the one-dollar note; Jefferson—the two-dollar note; Lincoln—the five-dollar note; Hamilton—the ten-dollar note; Jackson—the 20-dollar note; Grant—the 50-dollar note; and Ben Franklin—the 100-dollar note. Also, most telling—the words <u>under God</u> were not inserted into <u>The Pledge to the Flag</u> (Pledge of Allegiance) until 1954. The original pledge, not authored until 1892, stated: *"One Nation, with liberty and justice for all."* Moreover, the declaration of *"In God We Trust,"* on the nation's currency today, was not placed there until 1957 after a special act of Congress. Upon reflection, it is not that surprising that the 9th U.S. Circuit Court of Appeals should rule that the nation's current pledge does not meet with the criterion established by the founding fathers, thereby, violating their intent and making it unconstitutional. Finally, it is clear that the Deistic founders of America were not just willing to speak with a forked tongue—but four of them at once! First, through their attestations about the "Divine Architect" and "Providence," as well as their affinity for a belief in a "Supreme Being,"—we must conclude that they believed in some form of deity. However, and second, this deity never appears to have been given a distinguishing name—at least not for public hearing. Third, these men would time after time express their aversion for the Christian religion—not to mention their out right rejection of the divinity of Christ Jesus. While, and fourth, encouraging their country's citizenry to embrace the Christian religion.

Popular Revolutionary Symbol

The Founding Fathers & Democracy

The Founders' Facade

Though widely lauded for the relentless pursuit of democracy—the truth is that for almost 200 years of colonial life—the British model, rule by the monarchy and aristocracy, would suit the gentry class of the colonies just fine.[6] Not only was the wealth that they obtained through the cruel enslavement of other human beings palatable to them—but they also had no problem living under a system that gave no more than 10% of the White male population any say whatsoever about its course![7] Further, in the years leading up to the Revolutionary War—not once did the landed gentry petition the crown for the right of every colonist to self-determination. Moreover, despite all of their lofty proclamations about the ills of "Taxation without Representation"—the founders would establish a government in which, though required to pay taxes, a plurality of the country's citizenry did not have the right to vote!

Quite frankly, it was not a sudden lack of English democracy that the founders were weary of—but the financial shackles that the British were placing on them. In a nutshell, the British had mandated that commerce in the colonies would be limited to the exporting of homegrown commodities and the importing of goods from Europe. By 1776, however, 10% of the White male population had come to control half the wealth of the colonies—and they were tired of the English government telling them what they could, and could not, do with it!

Atop this, putting a stop to the crown's authority would add to their wealth through the elimination of English taxes. From discord over the right of British custom agents to search

---

[6] Colonial America, Collier's Encyclopedia Vol. VI, pp. 745 - 747 & Colonial Life, The Encyclopedia Americana Vol. VII, p. 281 & Colonial Life in America, The World Book Encyclopedia Vol. III, p. 1562
The system of class was no less prevalent in Britain's colonies than it was at home. The classes were thus: the Indentured Servant or Slave class, which essentially consisted of the poorest immigrants, criminals, and kidnapped Africans; the Meaner Sort class, although consisting largely of unskilled laborers, these people were not bound to any particular service; the Middling Sort class was made up of farmers, craftsmen, and shopkeepers; and finally the class of the Gentry, who were wealthy merchants, planters, and high office holders. In passing, it is not uncommon to find the term Esquire placed after their name.
[7] Colonial Life, The Encyclopedia Americana Vol. VII, p. 281

The Founding Fathers & Democracy

merchants for contraband, to the colonists' vehement rejection of the Sugar, Stamp, Townsend, and Quartering Acts—it is clear that economic issues were at the core of the conflict.[8] Indeed, the financial versus democracy motivation for the Revolutionary War is manifest, as although winning the war—<u>no discernible change in the governmental standing of the majority of the populace was even to be hinted at during the establishment of the nation</u>! To quote Hoffer:

> *"One can see that rudimentary principles of Rule of Law infused the first state and federal constitutions and the Bill of Rights. Even so, the language of the constitutions masked the political exclusion of certain groups. Indians, women, blacks, Catholics and Jews, and other disfavored groups did not gain equal rights with free white propertied males of the Protestant [or Deistic] faith . . ."*[9]

If the truth is to be told, the founders' disdain for equity amongst the classes is quite clear. For example, Alexander Hamilton is known to have referred to the common people, or 90% of the population, as *"beasts."* We also find Benjamin Rush being quoted as referring to the typical White settler as *"scum."*[10] In all fairness, Hamilton and Rush were not the only

---

[8] <u>Chronicle of America</u> p. 117, 122, 124, 125, 128, 131, 133, 137, 139, 143, 154, 180, 203, 228, 234, 236 & Fresia, J., <u>Toward an American Revolution</u> p. 25, 32 & Taxation, <u>World Book Encyclopedia</u> Vol. XIX, p. 54
The citizenry of the early nation was subject to excise taxes and tariffs. In general terms, a tariff is a tax on goods that are imported or exported, while an excise tax is a duty placed on an item of enjoyment or garnered from one's occupation.

[9] Tatch, J., <u>Freemasonry in the Thirteen Colonies</u> p. 13 & Hoffer, P., <u>Law and People in Colonial America</u> p. 123 & <u>Chronicle of America</u> p. 181 & Kick, R., (ed.), <u>YOU ARE BEING LIED TO: The Disinformation Guide to Media, Historical Whitewashes and Cultural Myths</u> pp. 214 - 215
Thomas Jefferson would publicly acknowledge the fact that some 10,000 free Blacks had fought valiantly against the British in the Revolutionary War. Despite this, the rights and happiness of the poor and disenfranchised, Blacks and Whites, were not primary concerns of the founders. In deference to Kick: *"It took over two years for the Bill of Rights to be introduced into the Constitution, and even then, it was partially a matter of power politics. The Anti-Federalists were against a strong government, not because they felt it would harm the civil rights of the landless and powerless, but because they did not want Congress to have direct authority to raise taxes . . . 'But they found that the more politically popular argument to use against ratification was the Constitution's lack of a Bill of Rights. So they advanced that argument, although it was a smokescreen . . .'"*

[10] Fresia, J., <u>Toward an American Revolution</u> pp. 2-3, 15-16 & Rosseau, J., <u>On the Social Contract</u> p. 18 & Rosseau, J., <u>The Social Contract</u> p. 51

members of the gentry class to belittle the lower class settlers; in actual point of fact, this view was widely held. Of course, one reason for this sentiment was that most of the colonists were from Europe's dispossessed classes; i.e., urban poor, orphans, prostitutes, and criminals. Yet, it is noteworthy that the founders did not mind the participation of this *"beastly scum,"* when it came to fighting wars and paying taxes.

However, James Madison would not stop with the mere disparagement of the common people; he would go so far as to depict access to government by the lower classes as a serious threat to the rich:

> *"The landed interest, at present, is prevalent, but in process of time . . . when the number of landholders shall be comparatively small . . . will not the landed interests be overbalanced in future elections? And unless wisely provided against, what will become of our government? In England, at this day, if elections were open to all classes of people, the property of landed proprietors would be insecure. An agrarian law would take place. If these observations be just, our government ought to secure the permanent interests of the country against innovation. Landholders ought to have a share in the government, to support these invaluable interests, and to balance and check the other. They ought to be so constituted as to protect the minority of the opulent against the majority."*[11]

Frankly, when it comes to democracy, the sentiments of the founders were in lock step with this declaration by John Jay, the first Chief Justice of the Supreme Court: *"The people that own the country ought to govern it!"*[12] Consequently, the *"We the People"* of the

---

Such sentiment was openly expressed by the wealthy of both sides of the Atlantic. In fact, The Social Contract of the heralded Rousseau states: *"Just as a herdsman possesses a nature superior to that of his herd, the herdsmen of men who are leaders, also have a nature superior to that of the peoples. According to Philo, Caligula reasoned thus, concluding quite properly from this analogy that kings were gods, or that men were beast."*

[11] Fresia, J., Toward an American Revolution p. 55 & Ketcham, R., James Madison: A Biography p. 229

[12] Fresia, J., Toward an American Revolution p. 32 & Jay, John, Grolier Multimedia Encyclopedia

Constitution's preamble was only meant to apply to the gentry and middling classes; with the aims of the latter being subordinate to the whims of the former. Everyone else, or the majority, was considered to be of no governmental import. In the words of Hamilton:

> *"All communities divide themselves into the few and the many. The firsts are the rich and well born, the other the mass of the people. The voice of the people has been said to be the voice of God; and however generally this maxim has been quoted and believed, it is not true in fact. The people are turbulent and changing; they seldom judge or determine right. Give therefore to the first class a distinct, permanent share in government. They will check the unsteadiness of the Second . . . Nothing but a permanent body can check the imprudence of democracy . . ."*[13]

The Republic

The nation's founders would settle for nothing less than a republic in which the power of the elite was insulated from the leveling effect of social equality. For every citizen to have the right to self-determination in their country was not even a consideration of the framers. A fact that is clearly illustrated by Franklin's proclamation at the conclusion of the Constitutional Convention—*"We have a Republic!"* Notice, Franklin did not say—*"We have a Democracy!"* Actually, as late as the creation of the Pledge of Allegiance (a hundred years later) the flag was still seen as a symbol of *"the republic, for which it stands."* Just so there won't be any confusion here, in general terms, any governmental system with laws (be they just or not) whose head official is not a king, can claim to be a republic. Thusly, <u>a republic and a democracy need not be one in the same.</u>

---

[13] Fresia, J., <u>Toward an American Revolution</u> p. 16 & Kick, R., (ed.), <u>YOU ARE BEING LIED TO: The Disinformation Guide to Media, Historical Whitewashes and Cultural Myths</u> p. 215
Scholars explain: *"The Founders themselves had no interest in anything more than a class democracy; their meetings were held in secret, and no reporters or information was allowed in or out of the hall during the proceedings. If one wasn't invited, one didn't count."*

The Founders' Facade

The framers first attempt at republic building was to establish the Articles of Confederation. The Articles of Confederation were modeled upon the deliberative governmental system of the six-member league of the native Iroquois nation: the Mohawks, Oneidas, Onondagas, Cayugas, Senecas, and the Tuscaroras. The driving principle of the Iroquois governmental structure was the belief that *"Reason would lead to Righteousness"*: an understandable position for men girded by truth. However, America's founders would soon grow to view the Iroquois model as restrictive and ill suited to achieve their goals.

Quickly characterized as not being strong enough to ensure the central control of the country by the powerful, the founders unilaterally dissolved the Articles of Confederation—whereby each state had equal representation and national action could not be taken without overwhelming consensus—for a government much more in line with that of their past. By instituting tiered government, they would make England's Parliament, Commons, Lords, and King their Congressional House of Representatives (to be checked as often as possible because it was closest to the common people), Senate (appointed by state legislatures until 1913), and Presidency. And, but of course, only a minority—or the *"well born"*--who had obtained or inherited property were allowed to participate. I guess we needn't be surprised considering that political power was long seen as a private possession of nobles in Medieval Europe. In truth, England's Magna Carta, which was formulated to curb the power of the king, provided no relief for commoners, or the majority of Brits, either.[14]

---

[14] Kick, R., (ed.), YOU ARE BEING LIED TO: The Disinformation Guide to Media, Historical Whitewashes and Cultural Myths pp. 74 - 75 & The World Book Encyclopedia Vol. IV, p. 2018, Vol. XVII, p. 8362 & Fresia, J., Toward an American Revolution pp. 9 - 11, 50, 54 & Articles of Confederation, Grolier Multimedia Encyclopedia & 200 Years: A Bicentennial Illustrated History of the United States Vol. I, pp. 161 - 162 & Wallace, P., The White Roots of Peace pp. 3, 9, 32 - 33, 45 & Universal Standard Encyclopedia Vol. II, p. 430, Vol. XIII, p. 4744 & The Encyclopedia of Discovery and Exploration p. 179 & The World of the Native American p. 133

The Articles of Confederation were the framework for government from 1781 - 1789. To avert war amongst themselves years before the arrival of the first colonists, the Iroquois chiefs resolved to unite into a confederation. As a declaration of the confederation's strength—the great Chief Deganawidah would state: *"I, Dekanawidah, and the Chiefs of the tribes in this League, now uproot the tallest pine tree and into the cavity left in the Earth we cast all weapons of war. We bury them from sight, deep in the ground, and plant again the*

The Founding Fathers & Democracy

Furthermore, from the beginning, the framers would establish a clear presidential cut out—the Electoral College. This gave their class the preeminent ballot in every election for the office of president. Accordingly, in a "democracy" of almost four million people—it would be a grand total of 138 wealthy individuals who would determine the country's first president: 69 choosing George Washington. A total of 132 electors (in a nation of millions) would return Washington to the presidency in 1792. As a matter of fact, the American populace was not even permitted to vote in the first eight presidential elections: the first popular vote for the office of president not taking place until the ninth presidential election in 1824. And, will wonders never cease—even though Andrew Jackson was to receive higher popular and electoral college vote tallies—we find John Quincy Adams ultimately being selected the nation's ninth president by the House of Representatives.

In several states the Electoral College voters were chosen by their legislatures. These "state representatives" were, and still are, not prohibited from voting differently than the people they represent. Indeed, on four separate occasions the Electoral College has chosen presidents who lost the country's popular vote—in 1824, 1876, 1888, and 2000. All of the framers' Electoral College moves were, of course, established under the guise of safeguarding democracy and ensuring the freedom of the people. Its clear that Voltaire's instruction *"to succeed in changing the multitude, you must seem to wear the same fetters,"* was not wasted on the nation's founding fathers.[15]

---

tree. Thus shall the great peace be established." In this confederation, issues were discussed annually and each tribe had a vote. Serious actions could not be undertaken before open debate had produced a unanimous vote.

[15] World Almanac and Book of Facts 2002 p. 376 & The Papers of George Washington: Electoral Count for the Presidential Election of 1789 (net) & Chronicle of America p. 202, 204, 209, 279, 280 & Congressional Quarterly Guide to U.S. Elections pp. 343 - 347 & Grolier Multimedia Encyclopedia - The American Presidency: Historical Election Results (net) & Popular Vote goes to Gore by 539,947 ballots Seattle P-I 12-22-00 p. A-3 & Seldes, G., The Great Quotations p. 650 & Donald, D., Lincoln pp. 259 - 260 & Chronicle of America p. 362, 382, 388 & Kelly, C., Conspiracy Against God and Man
Remarkably, in both of his elections for the Presidency—Abraham Lincoln believed that even if he carried the popular vote—the Electoral College would reject him. Lincoln considered the electoral vote *"the most dangerous point"* in the American election process. Incidentally, Voltaire was one of the most influential Freemasons in of his day.

The Founders' Facade

Now what was that famous remark by Aristotle—oh' yeah: *"He who thus considers things in their first growth and origin, whether a state or anything else, will obtain the clearest view of them."* Let's take a moment to do that:

- The founding fathers' Constitution did not allow poor White males the right to vote—that being left up to indifferent state legislatures.

- The document did not permit its Black male citizens the legal right to vote until 1867—not to mention the fact that in its original form a Black citizen was only considered to be 3/5 of a person.

- The document did not give women, of any color, the legal right to vote until the passage of the 19th Amendment in 1920 (some 140 years after the country's founding).

- Before the McCarran-Walter Act of 1952—Asian immigrants were barred from becoming citizens of the United States.[16]

- Finally, there were no provisions in the Constitution addressing past wrongs, granting citizenship, or which sought to prohibit future atrocities against the Native American.

Little wonder Supreme Court Justice Thurgood Marshall should state the following about the democracy and constitution of the founding fathers of America: *"The government they*

---

[16] Ropes, L., Aristotle p. 248 & Dictionary of American History Vol. IV, p. 209, Vol. V, p. 97, Vol. VII, p. 208 & Demott, B., Freemasonry in American Culture and Society p. 282 & Historical Statistics of the United States p. 9 & Ragsdale, L., Vital Statistics of the Presidency: Washington to Clinton p. 99 & United States Constitution, The World Book Encyclopedia Vol. XVII, p. 8362, 8372 & Chronicle of America p. 397, 398, 407, 409, 588 & Altman, S., The Encyclopedia of African-American Heritage p. 30 & Rosen, R., A Short History of Charleston p. 115 & Milele, N., The Journey of the Songhai People p. 178 & Hoffer, P., Law and People in Colonial America p. 123

It does not appear that the restriction of propertied voting was lifted nationally for poor White males until 1860. Although 10,226,000 White males lived in the country by 1850, only 3,161,830 total votes were cast in the 1852 election for president. Of course, the right of Blacks to vote has faced White obstruction; i.e., the Grandfather Clause, the Black Codes, denying state residency though granting American citizenship, the Klan, etc. Even worst, in a Georgia newspaper of 1868 we find, 28 Negroes lose seats in Georgia house: *"The Georgia legislature has expelled all 28 of its members on the grounds that a Negro has the right to vote in Georgia but not to hold public office. Opponents of the move warned this could cost Georgia its place in the union . . ."* The democratic failings of the nation are so glaring that Hoffer would be compelled to explain: *"Only when the rules and the reality come together does the Rule of Law become more than an apology or a masquerade . . ."*

devised was defective from the start, requiring several amendments, a civil war, and momentous social transformation to attain the system of constitutional government, and its respect for the individual freedoms and human rights, that we hold as fundamental today."[1]

Next, the tax burdens placed upon the White middling class by the founders after the Revolution, were just as repressive—if not more—than the crown's had been! But, like Abraham Lincoln said, *"You can't fool all of the people all of the time."* Thus, shortly after the war, there were many public demonstrations and martial actions taken against the policies of the founders. Yet, hardly willing to seriously consider the concerns of the middling class dissenters—who after all, were only Revolutionary War veterans who were losing their farms and unable to feed themselves—the gentry decided that their government needed the legal right to crush all protesters: remember, "*The people that own the country ought to govern it!*"

After several clashes, eventually, the concerns of the middling class would give way to the will of the gentry.[18] Little wonder that Professor Jerry Fresia should characterize the republicanism of the founders as follows:

> *"They wanted, in short, the 'essence of the British imperial system restored in the American states.' And in the name of the people they engineered a conservative counter-revolution and erected a nationalistic government whose purpose in part was to thwart the will of 'the people' in whose name they acted."*

---

[18] Fresia, J., Toward an American Revolution pp. 33 - 34 & Chronicle of America p. 136, 189, 190, 198 & Shay's Rebellion, The American Peoples Encyclopedia Vol. XVII, pp. 551 - 552 & Bartlett, J., Familiar Quotations: A Collection of Passages, Phrases, and Proverbs Traced to Their Ancient and Modern Sources p. 451 & Kick, R., (ed.), YOU ARE BEING LIED TO: The Disinformation Guide to Media, Historical Whitewashes and Cultural Myths p. 215
Although revolts against the elitist policy went back at least as far as 1764 (with the Regulators of North Carolina) the most noted revolt against the financial policies of the new nation's gentry was the Shay's Rebellion of 1786 in Massachusetts. Incidentally, Lincoln's whole quote is, *"It is true that you may fool all the people some of the time; you can even fool some of the people all the time; but you can't fool all of the people all of the time."*

Facade

In light of the fact that that the founding fathers expressly set out to establish a government that would *"protect the minority of the opulent against the majority,"* and give *"the rich and well-born"* a *"distinct, permanent share in government"* that would *"check the unsteadiness"* of the common people—some of you might be wondering why so many Americans believe that these men cherished democracy. Be well told, the framers understood that the class that controlled the country's newspapers and schools would be in the best position to form public opinion—<u>whether true or false</u>.

In the United States, the media and schools have historically been under the umbrella of the wealthy. Accordingly, from a very early point in the nation's history, the wealthy have made a point of telling the masses that what's good for the rich is great for the nation. Conversely, what's good for the poor is not only bad for the nation, but is a threat to the fabric of Western Civilization! Thusly, being a "Good American" has come to mean that if the millionaires and billionaires who control the six o'clock corporate news aren't concerned about it—surely, you don't need to worry about it! The situation is best summed up by Derrick Jensen who explains that the media's principal source of income is the 100 billion dollars a year American corporations spend on advertising; hence, in effect, one hand is simply washing the other. It's rather hard to dispute his conclusion considering that much of what you see on the nightly news is nothing more than press releases that have been spoon fed to them by corporate PR firms . . .

Merriam-Webster defines a <u>façade</u> as *"a false, superficial, or artificial appearance or effect."* Just so that you will be clear, allow me to close here with these words from Book

The Founding Fathers & Democracy

Three of Aristotle's Politics:

> *"The real difference between democracy and oligarchy is poverty and wealth. Wherever men rule by reason of their wealth, whether they be few or many, that is an oligarchy, and where the poor rule, that is a democracy . . ."*[19]

Scene at the Signing of the Constitution
by Howard Chandler Christy — 1940

---

[19] Fresia, J., Toward an American Revolution pp. 44 – 45 & (Video), Book TV: In Depth- Gore Vidal C-Span & Kick, R., (ed.), YOU ARE BEING LIED TO: The Disinformation Guide to Media, Historical Whitewashes and Cultural Myths p. 368 & Seldes, G., The Great Quotations p. 261 & Bill Moyers' Address: Inequality Matters (net) & Greider, W., Secrets of the Temple: How the Federal Reserve Runs the Country p. 39 & Signing of Constitution – *Courtesy of Teaching Politics* (net)

In an address on inequity, tax cuts, and class warfare—Bill Moyers explains that the gap between the rich and poor has grown to the highest level since the fifties: *"In 1960, the gap in terms of wealth between the top 20% and the bottom 20% was 30 fold. Four decades later it is more than 75 fold."* William Greider would observe the following about the structure of real wealth in the United States: *"The ladder of wealth looked like this: at the top were the 10 percent of American families that owned 86 percent of the net financial worth. Next came the 35 percent of families that shared among them the remaining 14 percent of financial assets. Below them were the majority, the 55 percent of American families that, on balance, had accumulated nothing. The 10 percent and, to a lesser degree, the larger group below them were, of course, the main customers for Wall Street investments . . ."*

The Founding Fathers & Democracy - Chapter Notes

[1] <u>Chronicle of America</u> p. 77, 96, 112, 119, 291, 308 & Quarles, B., <u>The Negro in the American Revolution</u> pp. 29, 141 - 142 & Marshall, T., <u>Commentary: Reflections of the Bicentennial of the United States Constitution</u> Harvard Law Review Vol. 101, Nov. 1987 pp. 1 - 2 & Pike, A., <u>Morals and Dogma of the Ancient and Accepted Scottish Rite of Freemasonry</u> p. 296

Though presentations of the savage Indians have been done to death, reports from White newspapers provide a clearer view of the nation's past; here is a brief sampling. An article of 1605 entitled, <u>European diseases decimating Indians</u> states: *"Disease has spread among the Indian populations like ripples in a giant pond. Epidemics of diseases such as smallpox, measles, dysentery, typhoid, tuberculosis and other European maladies are initiated at contact points along the coast of both continents and then spread inland by trade and by warfare, destroying millions of native inhabitants, sometimes before they have as much as much as set eyes on a white man . . ."* In 1676, the Nova Scotia reported, <u>An Indian lament</u>: *"As the white man pushes farther and farther into the forest that once belonged to the Indian, the native culture is being eroded, even destroyed. One chief responded to French criticism of Indian ways by saying 'We are very content with the little we have . . . if France, as you say, is a little terrestrial paradise, are you wise to leave it?'"* In 1725, we find, <u>Indian scalps sold in New Hampshire</u>: *"Captain John Lovewell, an Indian hunter, and his men paraded 10 scalps atop poles in Dover last February. They left town 1,000 pounds richer, the first men to capitalize on the 100-pounds-per-scalp bounty that has been offered by England. Yesterday, Lovewell led another hunt for Pigwacket Indians near Ossippe Lake. But this time, Chief Paugus and his warriors surprised them. Outnumbering the frontiersmen nearly two to one, the Indians surrounded the Lovewell encampment and avenged the scalpings. After a brutal encounter, Lovewell, many of his men as well as Chief Paugus were dead in a sea of blood."* A colonial newspaper of 1763 reports, <u>Killing Indians by smallpox proposed</u>: *"Informed sources say General Jeffrey Amherst, British commander of colonial forces on the Great Lakes frontier, recently wrote a vice commander, Colonel Henry Bouquet, advising him to try to inoculate Chief Pontiac's rebellious Indians with smallpox by means of infected blankets . . ."* In 1756, Peter Wraxhall, Secretary to the Indian Commissioner, explained that it was the constant claims by colonists to lands that they had no right, which was the greatest cause for conflict with the Natives. I can't help but be reminded of the Moslem witticism of centuries past: *"Don't worry, your things will be safe where you've place them—there are no Christians here."* A Washington D.C. article of 1830 entitled, <u>Removal Act exiles Indian tribes to West</u> states: *"Indian tribes are likely to be swept west of the Mississippi under the Indian Removal Act signed into law today by President Andrew Jackson. Passage of the legislation was accompanied by some of the most acrimonious debate ever seen in Congress, with critics claiming the bill was inhuman while proponents said it was the only way to save Indians from extinction. Under the law, Indians will receive perpetual title to Western lands, along with financial* assistance and a government guarantee of security. Although the act does not mandate the surrender of Eastern lands . . . Passage of the bill was a triumph for Jackson, a staunch nationalist who has made no secret of his desire to drive the Indians west. After taking office last year, the President urged the Creek tribe to cede its lands and head west, noting, 'Your white brothers will . . . have no claim to the land and you can live upon it, you and all your children, as long as the grass grows or the water runs, in peace and plenty'—" Yet, this final article fairly well sums up the experience of interaction between the Native American and Europeans. A Missouri paper of 1838 explains, "The Trail of Tears": 18,000 Cherokees driven from homelands: "*The forced removal of the Cherokees, mainly from Georgia, to the Indian Territory west of the Mississippi, is about to be completed. The removal process began October 1, and is expected to be concluded in early spring. The United States Army is conducting the transfer operation under General Winfield Scott. The forced removal policy has been roundly denounced by most humanists and constitutional experts. While the Supreme Court has essentially ruled that the Indians had the legal right to remain at their ancestral homes in Georgia, President Jackson did not feel that way. After hearing former Chief Justice John Marshall's verdict, he reputedly said, 'He has made his decision; now let him enforce it.' Whereupon Jackson ordered the army to move the Indians out of Georgia. Reliable witnesses say that as many as 18,000 Indians are being sent through the summer heat, droughts and winter snows to the Indian country. They also say that many of the Indians are dying of starvation, heat-induced diseases and exposure from the cold. An epidemic of smallpox is also reportedly decimating their ranks. General Scott has announced that he intends to conduct this operation with as little bloodshed and hardship as possible. The Indians, however, have already termed this long journey 'The Trail of Tears.'*"

Native Americans welcoming Europeans during the 1700s
Courtesy of Dr. William J. Ball - Teaching Politics

The Free-Masonic Foundations of These United States

The FreeMasonic Foundations of These United States

Today, the supporters of modern Freemasonry in America portray it as little more than a lighthearted fraternity that can occasionally be instrumental in the material benefit of its membership. However, historically speaking, the clergy and scores of leaders would vehemently oppose the men of this practice. For example, France, Portugal, and Spain would go so far as to ban the secret fraternal orders (Secret Societies) within their borders. Eastern Europe's communist block would also take a firm stance against such organizations. We even find Adolph Hitler going so far as to have German Freemasons put to death in the Third Reich![20] So, the question becomes—Why is there such a divergence of opinion about Freemasonry? Mindful here of Aristotle's instruction about the nature of a thing, let's begin our query with the craft's origins.

Ancient Masonry

The ancient Egyptians were the first people to establish a ceremonious Masonic system. De Lubicz explains that masons were heralded in Egypt as early as the 1st Dynasty (c.3100 B.C.); in fact, many considering the great African Temple at Luxor to be the world's first Grand Masonic Lodge. The association was created by Egypt's skilled stone (masonry) craftsmen. Held in high esteem by the Egyptians, these workmen would play an indispensable role in the civilization. You see, these wonderful artisans were the instruments of god who created the land's holiest monuments: Egypt's pyramids and tombs

---

[20] Freemasonry, Man, Myth & Magic Vol. VII, p. 951 & Inside the Third Reich: Memoir by Albert Speer p. 33 & Roper, H., Hitler's Secret Conversations 1941 - 1944 p. 152 & UK: The Craft BBC Online Network (net) & Hall, A., Strange Cults pp. 58 - 59 & Coil, H., Comprehensive View of Freemasonry p. 144 & Bullough, V., Homosexuality: A History pp. 90 - 96 & Lewy, G., The Church and Nazi Germany p. 24, 169 - 173, & Gypsies, The World Book Encyclopedia Vol. VIII, p. 451 & Gypsies: Wanderers of the World pp. 58 - 75 & The German economy and the Jews, Encyclopaedia Britannica Online
FYI: Hitler did not merely send Europeans who worshipped Judaism to the concentration camps. According to Albert Speer and many others—in the Third Reich Jews, Freemasons, Roman Catholics, Homo-Sexuals, Jehovah Witnesses, Social Democrats, Communists, and Gypsies were all persecuted. In actual point of fact, more than one out of every three people that the SS killed was not Jewish.

functioning as celestial incubators for deceased royalty—with temples serving as shrines for their deities! Hence, unlike today, the masons of ancient Egypt were considered to be agents of the heavenly god on the earth.[21]

Even while a precise understanding of the craft's methodology has not been acquired, scholars can credibly state the following: (1) they were highly trained in astrology; (2) they possessed a great degree of knowledge in the material craft of stone masonry; (3) they were versed in the natural laws and spiritual workings of the creation; and (4), they were Operative Masons (craftsmen who constructed monuments in stone).[22] In addition, we know that these African masons underwent demanding physical and spiritual trials before being accepted into the craft! For instance, circumcision was mandated for all members. We also find training being administered by degree; for example, Peter Tompkins points out: *"In the sixth, or penultimate, grade, the initiate was shown that the 'gods' of the Egyptians were the principles of life and the workings of universal law . . ."*[23]

---

[21] De Lubicz, R., Sacred Science: The King of Pharaonic Theocracy p. 143 & Tatch, J., Freemasonry in the Thirteen Colonies pp. 4 – 5 & Leadbeater, C., The Hidden Life in Freemasonry & Tompkins, P., The Magic of Obelisks p. 450, 454 & ben-Jochannon, Y., Black Man of the Nile and His Family pp. 252 - 253 & David, R., The Egyptian Kingdoms p. 86 & Budge, E.A., A History of Egypt Vol. II, pp. 43, 62 - 63, Vol. IV, pp. 106 - 110 & Montet, P., Lives of the Pharaohs p. 127 & Gardiner, A., Egypt of the Pharaohs p. 209 & James, G., Stolen Legacy p. 33
A title of the Egyptian Priest Hesy was Carpenter and Mason of the Golden Palace. What's more, scenes from the Temple of Khnum at Elephantine depict Egyptian Masons in Masonic attire. One of Egypt's most highly regarded Masons was the Royal Architect Amenhotpe of the 18th Dynasty. Serving Amenotep III, Amenhotpe would assist his king in material, and ethereal, matters.

[22] Higgins, G., Anacalypsis Vol. II, pp. 719, 768 - 769 & Hall, M., The Secret Teachings of All Ages & Tompkins, P., The Magic of Obelisks pp. 113 - 114, 337, 452 - 453 & Hall, M., Masonic Orders of Fraternity pp. 86 - 89 & ben-Jochannon, Y., Black Man of the Nile and His Family pp. 209 - 212 & Melton, J., Magic, Witchcraft and Paganism in America
The Crata Repoa, kept in Scotland, is said to be the oldest document to furnish information about Egyptian masonry.

[23] Higgins, G., Anacalypsis Vol. I, p. 724, Vol. II, p. 65 & Tompkins, P., The Magic of Obelisks p. 114, 121, 124, 340 & Baptism, Encyclopedia of Religion Vol. II, p. 60 & Janssen, R.M., & J.J., Growing Up in Ancient Egypt pp. 90 - 91 & Burn, A., & Selincourt, A., Herodotus: The Histories pp. 167 - 168 & Murphy, E., Diodorus on Egypt p. 35 & Bunson, M., A Dictionary of Ancient Egypt p. 53
The earliest form of Baptism was probably the dunking of Egyptian initiates in the Crater of Nous. The immersion was symbolic of passing from death to life, in preparation for the

The greater the knowledge and skill level of the Masonic craftsman—the greater his rank. Of all the grades in Egyptian masonry, the highest was Grand Master. And it was the Grand (or Master) Mason, who supervised the country's great work projects.[24] The ultimate goal of Egyptian masons appears to have been to possess perfect knowledge so that they would be excellent craftsmen for the gods and great servants to their pharaoh . . .

Medieval Masonry

Moving from the Operative Masonry of the ancient Egyptians, we come to that of Medieval Europe. While the history of Masonry in the Middle Ages is rather sketchy—it is fairly clear that this period would ultimately give rise to a different type of institution. This is manifest insomuch as many of the philosophical cornerstones of Medieval and modern masonry did not exist in the times of early dynastic Egypt: King Solomon's temple, for example. According to Coil:

"Not a great deal is known of the customs of the operative freemasons of the 16th century and earlier centuries . . . They recognized a community of interests in their mystery; they insisted upon honest workmanship and a fair degree of morality; and they aided each other by instruction . . . The art had to be learned by precept and example and transmitted orally, for books upon such subjects hardly existed. The general illiteracy of the age was, however, of advantage to the freemasons by

---

reception of the holy instruction. Weisse and Gorringe explain that nine initiatory trials were depicted in the Temple of Seti I. Parenthetically, circumcision was probably no extra hardship for masons as the procedure was commonly associated with cleanliness and widely performed before the period of male adolescence in ancient Egypt.

[24] ben-Jochannan, Y., <u>Black Man of the Nile and His Family</u> p. 258 & Uphill, E., <u>Egyptian Towns and Cities</u> p. 24 & Casson, L., <u>Daily Life In Ancient Egypt</u> p. 13 & Hall, M., <u>The Secret Teachings of All Ages</u> pp. LXXVII - LXXVIII, CLXXXIII & <u>The Kybalion: Hermetic Philosophy</u> p. 16 & Tompkins, P., <u>The Magic of Obelisks</u> p. 121, 340

The ranks were thus: (1) a neophyte was someone newly initiated; (2) a hierophant was a priest who conducted a ceremony; (3) an adept was someone who had mastered knowledge of the Philosopher's Stone; and (4), the final class was Grand Mason.

The Founders' Facade

enabling them to control or even monopolize the secrets of their art and to select those to whom it was thought proper to communicate it."[25]

In brief, 12th century France had a number of organized groups of craftsmen who worked with stone. These independent and migratory guilds developed cryptic signs and phrases to maintain their exclusivity and substantiate rank. After a while, these workmen would be known as *macon* in France, which means "builder of walls." By the 13th century, similarly structured guilds of stone craftsmen and carpenters were established in many parts of Europe. These artisans were employed by the Church and the wealthy to build their cathedrals and castles. However, Manly Hall would observe, *"They made themselves independent of the Church, and in the thirteenth century they formed an extensive building association . . . having lodges . . . at Strasbourg, Vienna, Cologne, and Zurich."*[26]

The Masonry of Europe would maintain this posture until the 16th century. Until this point, Europe's Masonic guilds were centered upon the material crafts and the preservation of their autonomy from the Church and the wealthy. Yet, during the 16th century, Europe's guilds decided that competence in the material crafts would no longer be requisite for membership.

---

[25] Morgan, W., Illustrations of Masonry, BY ONE OF THE FRATURNITY, WHO HAS DEVOTED THIRTY YEARS TO THE SUBJECT p. 35 & Coil, H., A Comprehensive View of Freemasonry p. 38

[26] Kelly, C., Conspiracy Against God and Man pp. 42 - 43 & Coil, H., Comprehensive View of Freemasonry p. 35 & Hall, M., Masonic Orders of Fraternity pp. 10 - 11 & Morgan, W., Illustrations of Masonry, BY ONE OF THE FRATURNITY, WHO HAS DEVOTED THIRTY YEARS TO THE SUBJECT p. ix & The Philosophical Research Society: Freemasonry (net) & Morey, R., The Truth About Masons pp. 60 - 69

The Italian word for Mason was Macio. Additionally, the highly regarded author and honorary 33 degree Mason Manly Hall tells us that the practices of these Medieval craftsmen were actually modeled after the Comacini Masters of ancient Italy. With the fall of the Roman College of Architects during the 4th century, the surviving membership is said to have escaped to the Isle of Comacini in Northern Italy. The Comacini are considered to be the artisans most responsible for the eventual creation of Lombard and Romanesque architecture. They divided themselves into three classes: the disciples, masters, and grand masters. The group is also said to have worn gloves and aprons, utilized secret passwords and signs, and assembled in places called Logia. In all fairness, many modern Freemasons take issue with this view of the craft's origins. The fact that there is no verifiable history of Comacini Masters is the basis for their position.

Shortly thereafter, the guilds would begin to admit men of high social standing into their ranks. Emmanuel Rebold writes:

> *"Queen Elizabeth, indignant that the Freemasons had not offered the Grand Mastership to her consort during his lifetime, on the 27th of December of this year, ordered the dissolution of the Masonic assembly which on that day commenced its semi-annual meeting, and ordered the execution of her edict to be enforced by a detachment of armed men; but, upon a report having been made to her by the commanding officer of the detachment expressive of the politically harmless character of the assembly, the Queen revoked her order. Subsequently Queen Elizabeth became the protectress of the Freemasons of her kingdom, and confirmed their choice of Thomas Sackville for Grand Master."*[27]

Free-Masons

Needless to say, with this shift in the social standing of its membership during the 16th century, the character and social import of Masonic guilds would change dramatically in Europe: the material crafts and the construction of cathedrals no longer being paramount. This is the age that gave rise to the <u>Non-Operative</u> (or Speculative) Mason. In time, these Non-Operative masons would come to be known as <u>Accepted</u> or <u>Free-Masons</u>.[28] Count Goblet d Alviella would characterize this change in masonry thus: *"Speculative Masonry is the legitimate off-spring of a fruitful union between the professional guild of Mediaeval*

---

[27] Hall, M., <u>Masonic Orders of Fraternity</u> p. 11, 43 & Kelly, C., <u>Conspiracy Against God and Man</u> p. 43
James I and Charles I are known to have been initiates of Freemasonry.
[28] Freemasonry, <u>Man, Myth & Magic</u> Vol. VII, p. 951 & Freemasons, <u>Encyclopedia of Religion</u> Vol. V, p. 417 & Kelly, C., <u>Conspiracy Against God and Man</u> pp. 42 - 43 & Hall, M., <u>Masonic Orders of Fraternity</u> pp. 10 - 11 & Coil, H., <u>Comprehensive View of Freemasonry</u> pp. 35 - 38
It is to be noted that Coil makes the argument that the term <u>Free-Mason</u> was actually used before the advent of Speculative Masonry.

The Founders' Facade

Masons and a secret group of philosophical Adepts, the first having furnished the form and the second the spirit."[29]

Yet, the fact that many Europeans believed this Speculative Masonry to be based upon such controversial foundations as rationalism, spiritualism, secrecy, and atheism—would cause these orders to be viewed with suspicion. For instance, during the 17th century, Oliver Cromwell would oppose the increase of Masonic lodges in England: declaring them the *"secret meeting places of the nobles."* But even while such sentiment was not hard to come by, Freemasonry faced little opposition as it had become a fixture amongst much of the upper crust of Western Europe. In fact, so much so that an international Masonic Congress was convened in Europe in 1663. One of the outcomes of this assembly was the establishment of the three degrees of Freemasonry: the Entered Apprentice (or Doers); the Fellow Craft (or Thinkers); and, the Master Masons (or Knowers). It was during this era that the masons would become a powerful political force in Europe.

The Order of the Templars

In the 1660's, French Freemasons would actually initiate a Masonic movement to avenge the Knight Templars: an effort that would not only call for an all out assault against the French and English monarchies—but the destruction of the Catholic Church as well![30] To provide you with a bit of historical background, 12th century conditions spawned by the

---

[29] Kelly, C., Conspiracy Against God and Man p. 43 & The Scottish Rite Journal (net)
Count Goblet d Alviella was a Grand Master of Belgian Freemasonry during the 19th century. As for his comment, though the latter has most certainly been an adherent of many of the ancient Mysteries—the argument is to be made that the count's eloquent characterization is, in fact, backwards.

[30] Kelly, C., Conspiracy Against God and Man p. 44 & Percival, H., Masonry and its Symbols p. 40 & Freemasonry, Man, Myth & Magic Vol. VII, p. 955
By the by, Duke of Albemarle George Monch, a Freemason, is said to have secretly worked to bring about Richard Cromwell's downfall despite appearing to serve him as a loyal advisor.

<u>The FreeMasonic Foundations of These United States</u>

Crusades would give rise to a Christian force in Europe known as the Knight Templars. They essentially were pious knights charged with performing two principal duties: first, to protect royal treasure and property; and second, to guard religious routes from Europe to the Holy Lands. Through time, the Templars' political awareness, intimate knowledge of royal monetary transactions, and their military prowess is said to have led these pious knights into vice and corruption.

Before long, the principal activity of the Templars had turned from their first calling to banking and making loans to Europe's nobility. Of course, those nobles who were unable to repay their debt lost their collateral: most commonly their land. Eventually, the Templars were to divide themselves into knights, chaplains, sergeants, and craftsmen who were only answerable to their grand master and a general council that only paid heed to the pope. Hence, secular rulers had no authority that the Templars were compelled to respect. Soon, the Templars would come to represent one of the wealthiest societies in Europe.

To stem the order's power and legally impound their wealth—Europe's royalty and clergy would mount an all-out assault against the Templars in the 14th century. The principal accusations against them were these: (1) secret initiations and utilizing signs known only to themselves; (2) rejecting the Christian Christ and cross; (3) altering Christian Mass; (4) exhibiting Eastern symbols and beliefs; (5) worshipping Baphomet (represented as a head or skull); (6) homosexuality; and (7), forming their own governing powers within the states of their residency so that they were only answerable to their Grand Masters.

King Philip IV of France and Clement V imprisoned and killed many Templars. Eventually, Italy, England, and Germany would disband the Templars in their lands. Thus, the Templars were not merely disbanded during the 14th century—their wealth and lands were seized—and scores of their brethren would lose their lives through execution! Incidentally, Spain and Portugal tried the Templars within their borders—but finding them innocent, allowed them to continue on as the orders of Montesa and Christ, respectively. Yet, it was these events that the French Freemasons of the 17th century were vowing to avenge. Thus, the beginning of Freemasonry's assault upon the monarchy and Catholicism . . .[31]

Freemasonry & Spiritualism

As if their oaths of secrecy, Deism, and their defense of the Templars had not supplied Europe's anti-Masonic Christian forces with enough ammunition—the Freemasons would then go on to sanction the use of Eastern mysticism! At the Masonic Congress of 1663, it was determined that beliefs held by the enigmatic Rosicrucians should officially be incorporated into Freemasonry. Although this group demonstrated more respect for the Christian religion than Freemasonry traditionally had—the beliefs of the followers of the Rosy Cross were formulated in alchemy, the Kabbalah, and that which is commonly associated with occult teachings. Interestingly, the Rosicrucians make little apology for this, maintaining:

"We freely admit our Oriental character, origin and modes of thought, and challenge the showing of any grand human idea that did not originate in Eastern

---

[31] Crow, W., History of Magic, Witchcraft and Occultism pp. 169 - 174 & Templars, Grolier Multimedia Encyclopedia & Knight Templar, Man, Myth & Magic Vol. XI, pp. 1482 - 1484 & Martin, E., The Trial of the Templars & Schwartz, T. & Empey, D., Satanism: Is Your Family Safe pp. 32 - 33 & Hall, A., Strange Cults pp. 50 - 51 & Whalen, W., Christianity and American Freemasonry pp. 142 - 143 & Kahaner, L., Cults that Kill & Hudson, H., The Story of the Renaissance p. 11 & (Video), The World of Joseph Campbell: The Story of Parzival W. Free 1989 & I John 4:2

I would probably be remiss not to share two quick observations by Hudson and Campbell, respectively. The former writes, *"Cases are on record of the conversion of Christians to the Moslem faith; it is significant in a more general way that the Knight Templars suffered much from their known sympathies with Saracenic [Moorish] ideas . . ."* As for the latter, Campbell believes that the castration of the Grail King during his fight with the Pagan Knight (who lost his life) in Eschenbach's Parzival, epitomizes the rift between the Templars and the Catholics. According to Campbell, the Western cardinals' compulsion to kill Nature, was the very act that would render their lives impotent. Rather remarkable, considering the scriptures explain that Yeshua was, *"God come in the flesh."*

lands. We claim to know the 'Grand Secret,' and to be able to teach mankind many things concerning the body, soul, will, prolongation of existence, and concentration of mental energy, never dreamed of by thinkers of colder latitudes . . ."[32]

Thus, the 17th century would usher in another great wave of transformation in the institution of Freemasonry. In Guiley's Encyclopedia of Witches & Witchcraft we find: *"The 17th and 18th centuries witnessed a popularity of secret magical orders, such as freemasons and Rosicrucians, whose rituals were based on the Hermetica, mystery schools, the tarot, interpretations of the Kabbalah and astrology."* Additionally, Whalen explains that Freemasonry combines parts of Mithraism, the Egyptian priesthood, the system of the Pythagoreans, Essenes, Cabalists, Druids, the orders of knighthood, Rosicrucians, Arabic Secret Societies, and the Knights Templar in its initiations and higher degrees.[33] This all said, we even find Freemasons embracing the idea of reincarnation. Little wonder that scholars should characterize the spiritual disposition of the craft as follows:

"Eighteenth century freemasonry . . . housed Newtonians, pantheists, materialists, and deists, with the specific identity of the object of worship revered at lodge

---

[32] Kelly, C., Conspiracy Against God and Man p. 44 & Crow, W., History of Magic, Witchcraft and Occultism pp. 216 - 221 & Randolph, P., Hermes Trismegistus: his Divine Pymander p. 6

[33] Guiley, R., Encyclopedia of Witches & Witchcraft p. 216 & Freemasonry, The New Catholic Encyclopedia Vol. VI, p. 132 & UK: The Craft BBC Online Network (net) & Morgan, W., Illustrations of Masonry, BY ONE OF THE FRATURNITY, WHO HAS DEVOTED THIRTY YEARS TO THE SUBJECT & Randolph, P., Hermes Trismegistus: his Divine Pymander p. 4

After comparing the designs of later practitioners with the clear and simple truths delivered by the ancients, Randolph explains: *"There is no form of human philosophy, so-called, that can hope to supersede these. If their influence is forgotten in the heat and turmoil of the younger life, the soberer years are sure to revive them with increased power. The most cultivated intellects cannot erect a new faith to take their place. These mental diseases that come but once in life,—known as speculation, free-thinking, rationalism, positivism, and the like,—may, like the mumps and measles of childhood, overtake us as we pass certain exposed stages of existence; but the old health of nature, invincible in her instincts and intuitions, comes back with redoubled strength, and the golden thread that we thought to be lost, draws all together, and life rounds out its inner experiences at last in harmonious and happy proportions. The philosophies and phantasms break up and disappear like exhalations of the mourning, and the sun shines bright and clear once more in the very face of the soul."*

meetings under the name of 'Grand Architect' . . . In effect, the eighteenth century freemason could worship Newton's God or Nature . . ."[34]

In view of these findings, it is not difficult to fathom the schism that had developed between Freemasonry and the Church. By the 1730s, Masonic leaders were being widely denounced by Catholics as dangerous occultists. To add fuel to the fire, the official Masonic Constitutions, written by James Anderson in 1723, would cast Freemasonry as a universal religion. Further, it was widely known that many masons on the continent, especially in France, were avowed atheists. Clergymen would also condemn passages in Baron Von Hund's The Rite of Strict Observance. Containing a number of remarkable admissions, a few of the most troubling to the anti-Masonic forces were these; (1) that many 13th century Templars escaped to Scotland and continued their order in secret; (2) that 18th century Freemasonry was a direct off-shoot of the Templars' craft; (3) that Freemasonry was not based upon a democratic model; and (4), that orders were strictly controlled by secret superiors who upon occasion utilized occult practices.

I cannot help but be reminded that Sir Godfrey Higgins, himself a freemason, would remark:
"Why do the priest led Monarch's of the continent persecute masonry? Is it because they are not entrusted with its secrets; or, because their Priests cannot make it subservient to their base purposes? All these are questions I may ask, gentle reader; But all I may not answer. If you be not satisfied, ask his Royal Highness the Duke of

---

[34] Kelly, C., Conspiracy Against God and Man pp. 46 - 47, 49 - 51 & Crow, W., History of Magic, Witchcraft and Occultism p. 275 & Demott, B., Freemasonry in American Culture and Society p. 11 & Schmidt, A., Fraternal Organizations p. 4 & Lindberg, R., & Number, R., God & Nature p. 248 & Boller, P., George Washington and Religion p. 94 & Bullock, C., Revolutionary Brotherhood: Freemasonry and the Transformation of the American Social Order 1730 - 1840 pp. 22 - 23 & The Crown and the Capitol - Anti-Masons (net)
Schmidt explains, *"The fraternal secret orders see the role and function as paramount. Ritual content is seen . . . as a necessary means of teaching moral values."* While George Washington often used the phrase Grand Architect—it appears that the Rosicrucians first popularized it. Finally, Newton would ascribe the origins of Masonry as Hebraic. He would also inflate the antiquity of the Jews and make erroneous associations between them and the Druids.

*Sussex: He can answer you **IF HE SO CHOOSES**. But this I may say, it is not every apprentice or fellow-craft who knows all of the secrets of masonry . . ."*[35]

The Great Coup d' Etat

No longer guilds of reclusive builders of shrines and cathedrals—these exclusive assemblies of wealthy and influential Freemasons were creating structures that most could not readily see—but that were nonetheless quite formidable. Up to this point, the ranks of Europe's anti-Masonic royalty and clergy had never been faced with such a domestic challenge. Indeed, the force of Masonry would become so strong in England that it was able to prevent James II from taking the throne upon the death of his brother Charles II in 1685. Kelly makes the following assessment of Freemasonry's influence upon the political environs of 17th century England:

> *"The fact is that around this time there developed in the ranks of the Masons strong anti-Stuart, anti-Church, and anti-Bourbon sentiments. So significant was this change that when Charles II died, the force of Masonry [successfully] moved to*

---

[35] Lindberg, R., & Number, R., God & Nature p. 247 & Coil, H., Comprehensive View of Freemasonry pp. 9 - 10 & Kelly, C., Conspiracy Against God and Man pp. 45, 72 - 74 & Schmidt, A., Fraternal Organizations pp. 6 - 7 & Kelly, C., Conspiracy Against God and Man pp. 63 - 65 & Crow, W., History of Magic, Witchcraft and Occultism pp. 274 - 275 & Hall, M., Masonic Orders of Fraternity pp. 68 - 69 & Melton, J., Magic, Witchcraft and Paganism in America p. 49 & Higgins, G., Anacalypsis Vol. I, p. 653 & Morgan, W., Illustrations of Masonry, BY ONE OF THE FRATURNITY, WHO HAS DEVOTED THIRTY YEARS TO THE SUBJECT pp. 39 - 40

Baron Von Hund founded the Order of the Rite of Strict Observance in Germany c.1750. Popular from its inception, the order spread into France, Switzerland, Italy, and Russia. Here, Morgan echoes the pronouncement of Higgins: *"Thus ends the first degree of Masonry, and the reader, who has read and paid attention to it, knows more of Masonry, than any Entered Apprentice in Christendom . . . for very few even attempt to learn the Lectures, or even the Obligations: They merely receive the degrees, and there stop, with the exception of a few who are fascinated with the idea of holding an office . . ."*

prevent the accession of James II . . . The non-Jacobite Masons who remained in England supported William of Orange . . ."[36]

Moreover, we find that it was in this corridor of time that English Freemasonry would begin to expand the numbers of its ranks: within a six-year period the number of lodges doubled in Europe from 63 to 126. Our author continues:

"In England, Masonry adopted an air of universal beneficence. Robinson wrote: 'It is not unlikely that this was an afterthought. The political purposes of the association being once obtained, the conversations and occupations of the members must take some particular turn, in order to be generally acceptable.' The Lodge of St. Paul at London made . . . an appeal for increased membership, saying that 'the privileges of Masonry should no longer be restricted . . .' But a much more important event in the history of Masonry stemmed from a meeting held at the Apple-Tree Tavern in the south of England in 1717. There occurred there what has been called 'the great <u>coup d' etat</u>,' when (the) Grand Lodge was founded, and Speculative Masonry . . . was established on a settled basis with a ritual, rules and constitution . . . it is at this important date that the official history of Freemasonry begins."[37]

By the middle of the 18th century, for many Europeans the matter was quite clear—Freemasonry was not only guided by wealthy men of a Deistic as opposed to Christian mind—but also, the nature of this Secret Society was not republican in the least! Building walls, though not of stone, Freemasons were seen as essentially being concerned with maintaining a feudalistic pyramid, or more precisely <u>obelisk</u>, that was impervious to the mandates of traditional religious doctrine and state government; hence the proclamation:

---

[36] Kelly, C., <u>Conspiracy Against God and Man</u> pp. 43 - 45 & Demott, B., <u>Freemasonry in American Culture and Society</u> p. 9 & Melton, J., <u>Encyclopedic Handbook of Cults in America</u> pp. 68 - 69

[37] Ibid.,

"The Lodge does not permit the State or Church to control its Activities."[38] At a ceremony held upon the completion of the Washington Monument, John C. Palmer would characterize Freemasonry thus:

> *"Masons are no longer builders of cathedrals and castles, 'Poems in Granite,' but of human society whose stones were living men. Their minds enlightened with divine truth, their hearts radiant with discovering the joy of pure love, their souls cherishing- like the ancient Egyptian worshippers of Osiris. The hope of immortality."*[39]

Desaguliers & 18th Century Freemasonry

By the end of 1700s, the ranks of Freemasonry had become a veritable Who's Who of wealth, influence, and nobility! The man who is accredited with being most responsible for this development is John T. Desaguliers. As an accomplished scientist, philosopher, and

---

[38] Kelly, C., Conspiracy Against God and Man p. 46 & Demott, B., Freemasonry in American Culture and Society pp. 9, 159 - 160 & Robinson, J., Proofs of a Conspiracy & The Freemasons: institutionalised parasites? (net)
It is explained that most members of the three degrees, the vast majority of the membership, will never gain entry into the thirty highest levels. One researcher explains: *"As novices they were Entered Apprentices. They were then 'passed' as Fellow Craft Masons and finally 'raised' as Masters. The very name has connotations of supremity . . . The 'Masters', who form the largest portion of Freemasons, are in most cases quite unaware of the thirty superior degrees to which they will never be admitted, nor even hear mentioned. This is the real picture, with the three lowly degrees governed by Grand Lodge and the thirty higher degrees governed by a Supreme Council."*

[39] Tompkins, P., The Magic of Obelisks pp. 336 - 337 & Demott, B., Freemasonry in American Culture and Society p. 162 & Morey, R., The Truth About Masons p. 61 & II Peter 2: 14
Try as one may, it is impossible to make genuine connections between the Masonry of the Egyptians and that of 18th century Europe. Even had the latter desired to follow the earlier craft, the relevant teachings available to them were, as yet, undeciphered. What's more, while the ultimate aim of Egyptian Masonry was to effect paths between man and the ethereal—Freemasonry's goals are centered much more upon corporeal gain and domination. How was Peter to phrase it: *"Greed is the one lesson their minds have learned."* Palmer's speech was delivered in 1885.

The Founders' Facade

lecturer—Desaguliers would become a court favorite; openly discussing the ideas of Newton and performing many scientific demonstrations for Europe's upper crust. In 1719, Desaguliers had become the Grand Master of Lodge No. 4. You might say he was Benjamin Franklin before Benjamin Franklin was. To quote Demott about Desaguliers:

> *"He was instrumental in bringing into the fraternity many men of nobility, and served as a liaison between Masonry and government. On November 5, 1737 he conferred the first two Masonic degrees upon Frederick, Prince of Wales. While in Edinburgh, Scotland on business, he was initiated into Scottish Masonry. He visited and sometimes took part in ceremonies in Holland and Paris. Desaguliers' successors as Grand Masters were of the Nobility; Dukes, Counts, Earls, Viscounts, a Marquess, and finally the Prince of Wales, who served from 1790 to 1813."*

It is rather apparent that Desaguliers' efforts were not in vain. Today, the British public is most weary of the secretive and co-opting influence of Freemasonry on their financial, legal, and governmental institutions. Yet, the question of Desaguliers' Freemasonry notwithstanding—he must be singled out for his contribution to European science during the 18th century. He is accredited with publishing more than 50 papers on optics, mechanics, and electricity! Desaguliers' most heralded work, however, was his Principia: a book that would have a profound influence upon the discipline of theoretical astronomy. But his greatest overall contribution might well have been his ability to translate relatively complex science into terms and devices that the feudal layman could grasp! He died in 1744, at the age of sixty.[40]

---

[40] Demott, B., Freemasonry in American Culture and Society pp. 4 - 5 & Schmidt, A., Fraternal Organizations p. 127 & World: Europe freemason report urges more openness BBC Online Network (net)
A B.B.C. world news report in May of 1999 explains: *"Members of the British parliament have urged the government to widen its campaign to reveal the identity of freemasons—a secretive society which is open only to men. In a Home Affairs Committee report, MPs demanded a clear deadline for members of the judiciary and the police to declare their interests in freemasonry. The Committee also called for the names of public office holders who had refused to declare whether they were freemasons to be published . . . The report was in response to a government pledge to force the society to be more open because of concerns of the widespread influence of freemasons in the legal field."*

The Illuminati

While much of the 18th century would be rosy for the masons, the public face of European Freemasonry would suffer another tremendous blow in 1776. During this year, Adam Weishaupt is said to have founded a group that he believed should be the archetype of Freemasonry—the Illumnati or "Light Bearers." Yet, though happenstance, several damaging papers were discovered which exposed the political aims of the Order of the Illuminati. The documents explained that—<u>from its inception the objective of the new Order would be to check the power of the Church and Governments—and to direct the affairs of the state</u>!

The papers also revealed how the Order planned to obtain these goals: (1) true obedience was to be equated with secrecy; (2) the ultimate aims of the Order would be kept from members of the lower grades, such that only those who had completely accepted their indoctrination would be allowed to rise; (3) the leadership would initiate their wishes through a series of men right beneath them, so that the underlings would never learn their actual identities: *"In this way I can set a thousand men in motion and . . . operate on politics"*; (4) blackmail to test, or keep members in line, would be permissible; (5) nothing that was associated with the Order should be referred to by its real name; (6) women were to be utilized against others to obtain the Order's goals; (7) educational and church hierarchies were professions to be infiltrated, and institutions of higher learning were to be formed by the Order; (8) the legal profession and military schools were to be infiltrated by the membership; (9) writers and reviewers were to be employed to advance the Order's goals; (10) if a writer was unsympathetic to their aims, he was first to be won over—if not, he was to be vilified; (11) the public mind was to be put at ease through open shows of popular and benevolent acts; and (12), the taking of lives was permissible to obtain the Order's goals.

Despite the discovery of their plan, incredibly, the Order managed to proceed with their program. By the early 1800s, the Illuminati's influence had spread to the countries of Italy, Venice, France, Austria, Poland, Denmark, Hungary, Russia, Sweden, Holland, Saxony, and America. According to Cahill: *"The Illuminists and other kindred secret societies were suppressed by the Bavarian Government . . . but their principles and methods, which got merged into Freemasonry, have continued even to our own day . . . and . . . spread . . . into every part of the known world."*[41]

---

[41] Crow, W., History of Magic, Witchcraft and Occultism pp. 274 - 275 & The Freemasons: institutionalised parasites? (net) & Schwartz, B., George Washington: The Making of an American Symbol p. 172 & Morey, R., The Truth About Masons pp. 108 - 109 & World: Europe freemason report urges more openness BBC Online Network (net) & Demott, B., Freemasonry in American Culture and Society pp. 20 - 22 & Kelly, C., Conspiracy Against God and Man pp. 46, 99 - 122 & Robinson, J., Proofs of a Conspiracy & The Address of the National Anti-Masonic Convention to the People of the United States pp. 4 - 5 & Books on Freemasonry: Antimasonic books & pamphlets from the 19th and early 20th century (net) & Kick, R., (ed.), YOU ARE BEING LIED TO: The Disinformation Guide to Media, Historical Whitewashes and Cultural Myths pp. 40 - 41 & & CounterPunch - CNN AND PSYOPS (net) & Turner, W., Rearview Mirror: looking back at the F.B.I., C.I.A., and other tails pp. 91 - 113

In passing, Weishaupt may well have been a Masonic agent of the long established Lodge of Theodore. That notwithstanding—If Weishaupt was an agent of French and German Masons, the Martinists and Illuminists respectively, his establishment of the Illuminati was quite probably the implementation of the ring's Plan of Arcesilaus. The Masonic grades of the Illuminati were thus: Nursery level was Preparation, Novice, Minerval, Illuminatus Minor; Masonry level was Apprentice, Fellow Craft, Master; and Mysteries level was Presbyter Priest, Prince Regent, Magus, and Rex. Note the similarity between goal number 9 and this remark by an anonymous C.I.A. official: *"One journalists is worth 20 agents."* Hardly surprising once reflecting upon Sun Tzu's The Art of War: *"All warfare is based upon deception."* Yet, considering the Illuminati's early concern with controlling education, writers, and reviewers—it would be naive not to conclude that a similar scheme would not exist in regard to music, cinema, and but of course—news and television programming. Hence, in essence, we are taught what's true and who to love by the agents of lies and hate. Shortly after the C.I.A's inception, the head of covert action would boast about the Agency's ability to sway public opinion anywhere in the world. And now, lo' and behold, Alexander Cockburn and Abe de Vries report that military personnel from the Fourth Psychological Operations Group based at Fort Bragg in North Carolina have, until recently, been assigned to CNN news headquarters in Atlanta. Finally, insomuch as I have already been approached—but ain't buying what their selling—the rest comes as no surprise . . .

Europe's Masonic Gulf

One quick aside here, as late as the 19th century, chasms would exist in British masonry. The most significant of these was the cleft between those who came to be deemed <u>Ancients</u> and those called <u>Moderns</u>. One underlying reason for the schism was probably due to the fact that the former were principally Irish. However, a consequence of the rift was that the Ancients would cultivate membership in the Army—the Moderns, the Navy.

In any event, in 1813 a union between the two orders was consummated. Regarding this Union, Coil remarks:

> *"After elaborate arrangements and the preparation of detailed articles of Union, the engineers of the reconciliation hit upon the sagacious plan of electing two royal brothers, the Duke of Sussex and the Duke of Kent, Grand Masters of the Moderns and Ancients, respectively. The Articles of Union having been signed by them and other representatives of the two branches, the hitherto rival bodies came together with the greatest good will . . . and, the two Grand Lodges having been opened in separate rooms, marched into the hall, forming a single body, presided over by the two Dukes. The Articles of Union were read and approved, and the Duke of Kent having withdrawn his name from consideration, the Duke of Sussex was unanimously chosen Grand Master of the 'United Grand Lodge of Ancient Freemasons of England.'"*[42]

---

[42] Demott, B., <u>Freemasonry in American Culture and Society</u> pp. 11 - 12 & Coil, H., <u>Comprehensive View of Freemasonry</u> pp. 110 - 111 & Percival, H., <u>Masonry and its Symbols</u> p. 42 & <u>By George What a City</u>! (net)
Coil explains that pure Ancient Masonry only had three degrees: Entered Apprentice, the Fellow Craft, and the Master Mason (which included the Supreme Order of the Holy Royal Arch). Incidentally, George III does not appear to have been a mason, but he certainly was surrounded by Moderns—from his father, to his brothers, and his sons. The Moderns (often

Freemasonry in Early America

Crossing the Atlantic, we find that the institution of Freemasonry would have no less a bearing upon the affairs of the gentry in the colonies than in Europe. In 1730, Daniel Cox was appointed the first Grand Master of the North American colonies. Shortly thereafter, the Immemorial Rights, Warranted, and Provincial Grand Orders were all to grant charters to lodges in North America; the earliest being issued in 1733. As in England, the membership of the Moderns tended to be a bit more aristocratic than that of the Ancients in the colonies.[43] In deference to Demott:

> *"The Masonry of England and Europe was primarily one of Nobility or persons of high standing in their communities. No doubt this situation existed in the Thirteen Colonies during the formation of the United States."*[44]

Truth be told, the Continental Congress was spawned in Colonial Freemasonry. The fact that George Washington's most trusted generals were freemasons, or brethren of the "Mystic Tie," is well established. Also, according to David Ovason, no less than 44 of the 56 signers of The Declaration of Independence were Freemasons. In the words of Sidney Morse:

> *"The idea of a Union of the American Colonies was first suggested by our first Provincial Grand Master, R∴W∴ Daniel Coxe, as a means of common defense*

---

seen as Tories) tended to favor the earlier Stuart monarchy and Church authority, while the Ancients (commonly seen as Whigs) sought to limit royal authority. After the American Revolution was over, large numbers of the Moderns left for Canada and England. The field was then left for the York and Scottish rites (via France and the West Indies) or the Ancients to dominate America.

[43] Coil, H., <u>Comprehensive View of Freemasonry</u> pp. 141 - 142 & <u>America Chronicle</u> p. 98
[44] Demott, B., <u>Freemasonry in American Culture and Society</u> p. 32
He goes on to say that Masonry's character would change in the U.S. with Western expansion: *"As the West was opened, however, people became Masons who were not of the 'upper class.' This is not to imply that carpenters, farmers and workmen are not worthy of membership, but merely to emphasize that the Craft was no longer one of nobility."*

against the Indians. It was again brought forward by R∴W∴ Benjamin Franklin, at the Albany Conference in 1750, when the danger of the French and Indian war seemed imminent. That menace having been averted by the conquest of Canada, the plan of Brothers Coxe and Franklin for a Colonial Union might never have been revived had the Mother Country adopted a policy of wise conciliation. It was the common danger to the liberties of the Colonist from the tyranny and oppression of the British Ministry, which brought about the Continental Congress."[45]

Having already discussed the actual disposition of the founders regarding Christianity, democracy, and the common settlers or *"beastly scum,"* the question becomes—<u>Was Freemasonry well-matched with these sentiments—and if so, could it be utilized to achieve their objective; i.e., a country ruled by wealthy White males under no obligation to answer to any spiritualist religion in any way whatsoever?</u> Frankly, having already seen that the Freemasons of Europe were not only powerful enough to openly oppose the Catholics and Protestants—but also thwart James II's succession to the throne—there can be no question as to the ability of the craft to influence a state's governing institutions. Atop this, it is clear that the Secret Orders spawned in feudal Europe were not the least bit concerned with democracy; indeed, routinely operating in direct opposition to it! Finally, the ranks of

---

[45] Colonial America, <u>Collier's Encyclopedia</u> Vol. VI, pp. 745 - 747 & Colonial Life, <u>The Encyclopedia Americana</u> Vol. VII, p. 281 & Colonial Life in America, <u>The World Book Encyclopedia</u> Vol. III, p. 1562 & Roth, P., <u>Masonry in the Formation of Our Government 1761 - 1799</u> pp. 8 - 10, 149 -164 & Ovason, D., <u>The Secret Architecture of Our Nation's Capital</u> p.75 & Tompkins, P., <u>The Magic of Obelisks</u> p. 309 & Morse, S., <u>Freemasonry in the American Revolution</u> p. vii, ix & Tatch, J., <u>Freemasonry in the Thirteen Colonies</u> p. 144 & Coil, H., <u>Comprehensive View of Freemasonry</u> pp. 148 - 149 & Bullock, C., <u>Freemasonry and the Transformation of the American Social Order 1730 - 1840</u> p. 114 & Barry, J., <u>Masonry and the Flag</u> pp. 1 - 2
Some believe that as many as 50 of the 56 signers of the document were Freemasons; however, such noted writers as Roth and Coil place the number of Masonic signers at about half of this total. Of course, one of the problems for chroniclers is that Masonic records of the Colonial period may not be complete in every instance. That aside, I should point out that many Freemasons of the colonies chose to remain loyal to the crown during the revolution. It is probably safe to conclude that the best known of these was Benedict Arnold. At the conclusion of the war, most of the loyalist Masons either returned to England or moved to Canada rather than remain amongst those whom they saw as traitors.

The Founders' Facade

European masonry were filled with Newtonians, pantheists, materialists, and Deists. And I have encountered nothing which would cause me to conclude that the Colonial gentry desired to break that mold.

Just briefly, the feudal rulers of Europe considered political power a private possession that was only to be shared amongst a small number of lords. Commoners could live on and utilize a noble's land—provided they served him as fighters, farmers, or workers—and paid his taxes. The lord of the manner, or members of his family, typically manned the courts of feudal Europe. Also, ruler's made a point of maintaining discord between the differing groups of his realm to keep them under his yoke: normally, the greater his insecurity, the more despicable his measures to ensure conflict. According to Blum:

> *"Under feudalism a mounted fighting man, the knight, held a land grant, called a fief or 'beneficium,' from his superior or feudal lord. The grant gave him the right to receive an income from a particular estate or manor. In return he became the lord's vassal and had to swear oaths of homage and . . . present himself for military service . . . Feudalism applied to the ruling (and fighting) classes of medieval society—perhaps 5 per cent of the population. Although the common man, typically a peasant, was affected by the feudal system, he was not a part of it . . ."*[46]

The influence of the feudal model upon the anti-democratic scheme of Freemasonry is evidenced through the fact that secret superiors monitor and strictly control the order's underlings. Its anti-democratic design is also indicated by the fact that the vast majority of membership of the craft will never enter the craft's thirty highest levels, or have any say in

---

[46] Blum, J., The European World: A History pp. 20 - 23 & Cantor, N., The Civilization of the Middle Ages pp. 195 - 196 & Visigoths, Collier's Encyclopedia Vol. XXIII, p. 174 & Goetz, H., Life in the Middle Ages p. 107 & Middle Ages, The World Book Encyclopedia Vol. XI, pp. 5042 - 5043 & Davis, C., Western Awakening Vol. II, p. 50 & Simons, G., Barbarian Europe pp. 147 - 160 & Byzantine Empire, The Encyclopedia Britannica Vol. II, pp. 699 - 700 & Hoyt, R., Life and Thought in the Middle Ages pp. 51 - 52, 55 & Middle Ages, The World Book Encyclopedia Vol. XI, p. 5043 & (Video), The Western Tradition: The Middle Ages Annenburg 1989

the institution's course. Even more, despite the fact the supporters of Freemasonry often portray it as nothing more than a benevolent brotherhood—dating to the time of the Templars in Europe—from early on, these organizations have widely been suspected of trying to establish secret government; i.e., a system functioning undetected by, and impervious to, the government of the country in which they reside! Lastly, as previously discussed—these suspicions would crystallize into serious accusations in 1776 with the discovery of secret documents that outlined the political objectives of the Masonic Order of the Illuminati!

So, if the question is—<u>Was Freemasonry well-matched with the founders view of class—and if so, could it be utilized to achieve their objective; i.e., a country ruled by wealthy White males under no obligation to answer to any spiritualist religion in any way whatsoever</u>? If you were so inclined, you could say Freemasonry fit the founders' aims like a glove . . .

America's Secret Society

By the late 18th and early 19th centuries, many Americans had also come to view Freemasonry as a threat to the democratic model. A damning leaflet of 1784 entitled—<u>Considerations on the Society or Order of the Cincinnati</u>, believed authored and anonymously distributed by a member of the Cincinnati, accused the order of endeavoring to establish a secret society of American patricians (nobility). The author, who was to refer to himself as Cassius, explained that the Order's charter provided that membership and station be based upon heredity and primogeniture. Cassius also took issue with the Cincinnati's sponsorship of the high ranking German Freemason General Friedrich Steuben and the fact that its membership was principally made up of military officers. Incidentally, early Masonic support for General Steuben in the colonies may well have been initiated by

The Founders' Facade

Provincial Grand Master Ben Franklin.[47]

Needless to say, Cassius' leaflet would spark a great public uproar—so many having just lost their lives in the cause of "*Liberty*." Unsurprisingly, as President-General of the Order of the Cincinnati, and coordinator of affairs between the Order and other Masonic groups—George Washington was quite upset by the pamphlet's disclosures. Flexner writes:

> "*The trumpet vociferated that what Washington regarded as the main objects of the society, the perpetuation of friendships and charitable fund, were only cloaks for a sinister plot . . . 'It is in reality and will turn out to be an hereditary peerage,' that would rivet on the American people 'an order of nobility.' The only hope for the preservation of the American Republicanism, Cassius believed, was the 'Extirpating' of the Cincinnati altogether. However, he doubted that this could be achieved, as <u>he saw demagogues whipping up every species of unrest until</u> 'The Sovereign People' marched like lambs to the abattoir [slaughterhouse] of an Aristocracy on the European model . . .*"[48]

---

[47] Flexner, J., George Washington and the New Nation Vol. III, pp. 63 - 68 & Jefferson p. 791 & Bullock, C., Freemasonry and the Transformation of the American Social Order 1730 - 1840 pp. 130 - 131 & Writings: Franklin pp. 426, 1084 - 1089, 1108 & Demott, B., Freemasonry in American Culture and Society pp. 15 - 16, 20 & Tatch, J., Freemasonry in the Thirteen Colonies p. 21

Henry Price, Provincial Grand Master of New England—whose post was granted by Lord Montagu, Grand Master of the Grand Lodge of England, had appointed Franklin Provincial Grand Master of Pennsylvania in 1734. While Franklin was to express concern over the hereditary ascendancy policy of the Order, he was not opposed to it otherwise. In actuality, Franklin would play a pivotal role in the formulation of the nation's military and social policies. Yet, that he should acquire a position of authority is rather extraordinary considering that he was never elected to public office. In Hall's The Secret Destiny of America we find: "*Though he was never President, never a military General, never a lawmaker, his influence over political figures, generals and law makers was immense. His power lay in the Secret Societies of which he was a member and of which he was Chief spokesman . . .*" In passing, Franklin's mother would oppose his involvement in Freemasonry and the fact that he was a Deist.

[48] Flexner, J., George Washington and the New Nation Vol. III, pp. 63 - 67 & Jefferson p. 791 & Demott, B., Freemasonry in American Culture and Society p. 17, 24 & Morse, S., Freemasonry in the American Revolution p. ix & Callahan, C., Washington the Man and the Mason & Lipson, D., Freemasonry in Federalist Connecticut 1789 - 1835 & Morgan, W., Illustrations of Masonry, BY ONE OF THE FRATURNITY, WHO HAS DEVOTED THIRTY YEARS

Public rumblings, notwithstanding, the Order of the Cincinnati was never disbanded or forced to make any meaningful change to its charter.[49]

The American Craft's Unveiling

The country's most ardent challenge to Freemasonry would begin a generation later in the 1820s and 30s. In July of 1826, John Stearns, a Mason who was to renounce his membership, wrote <u>An Inquiry Into the Nature and Tendency of Speculative Masonry</u>. Stearns explained that Freemasonry was being utilized as a religious substitute for Christianity. Further, the one time Mason told his readers that the institution functioned as a government within government. Stearns would also discuss the influence of the Illuminati upon American Freemasonry. Vaughn writes, *"He led the way in expounding the theory that Masonry was a state within a state and that one day Masons would overthrow the*

TO THE SUBJECT p. 89 & Lyon, V., <u>Domestic Surveillance: The History of Operation CHAOS</u> Covert Action Information Bulletin ISS. 34 Summer 1990
Cassius is thought to have been Chief Justice Aedanus Burke of South Carolina. Apparently, Washington was initiated into Freemasonry at the Fredericksburg Lodge in 1752, which was formed under the Ancient Order of England. Demott adds: *"Much has been written about Washington's Masonic activities and the fact that his generals were also of the Craft. No doubt these officers were selected for their exhibited military skill, but 'The Mystic Tie' might have given Washington a little more confidence in those whom he did choose . . ."*
Incidentally, <u>Chaos</u> is the word that's uttered by Mark-Master Masons to indicate distress. Lastly, be it sheer coincidence or not—the CIA, with assistance of numerous government agencies, carried out an illegal domestic spy program. From the 50s through the 70s, they spied on thousands of Americans and the program was known as <u>Operation Chaos</u>.
[49] Flexner, J., <u>George Washington and the New Nation</u> Vol. III, p. 68 & Mills, C., <u>The Power Elite</u> p. 275 & (Video), <u>Book TV: In Depth - Gore Vidal</u> C-Span & <u>Matthew</u> 6:21
One cannot help call Cassius's warning to mind once reflecting upon this characterization of American government by Mills: *"The warlords have gained decisive political relevance. And the military structure of America is now in considerable part a political structure. The seemingly permanent military threat places a premium on the military and upon their control of men, money, and power; Virtually all political and economic actions are now judged in terms of military definitions of reality . . ."* According to Vidal, more than <u>seven trillion dollars</u> have been spent by the military industrial complex since 1949. I am reminded of the scripture that explains you will know where their hearts are when you know where they place their treasure.

democratic government of the United States and would crown one of their 'grand kings' as ruler of this nation."[50] Striking a nerve with the populace, Stearns' book went through five printings in three years; however, nothing would cause a greater public furor against American Freemasonry than the William Morgan affair.

In 1826, Royal Arch Mason William Morgan decided he would write a book entitled, <u>Illustrations on Masonry, By One of the Fraternity Who Has Devoted Thirty Years to the Subject</u>. In passing, some dispute whether Morgan had a right to claim the Masonic level of Royal Arch. That notwithstanding, in March of 1826, Morgan formed a partnership with John Davis, Russell Dyer, and fellow Mason David Miller. Their agreement was that Morgan would write the book and the others would see to its publishing; each man to receive one-fourth of the profits. In the text's Introduction we are warned:

> *"Masonry is to the modern world what the whole of Babylon was to the ancient; and is the beast with seven heads and ten horns, ready to tear out our bowels, and 'scatter them to the four winds of heaven.' Masonry gives rouges and evil-minded characters an opportunity of visiting upon their devoted victim, all the ill attending combined power, when exerted to accomplish destruction. It works unseen, at all silent hours, and still secret times and places; and like 'death' when summoning his diseases, pounces on its devoted subject, and lays him prostrate in the dust. Like the great enemy of man, it has shown its cloven foot, and put the public upon its guard against its secret machinations."*

Once word got out of the impending publication, Morgan faced threats of violence from the Freemasons; attacks were also made against the printers. To quote a passage from <u>The Address of the National Anti-Masonic Convention to the People of the United States</u>:

> *"To assist in publishing the secrets of freemasonry, a printer was employed. Against him, the malice of the fraternity was conspicuously displayed. While*

---

[50] Vaughn, W., <u>The Anti-Masonic Party in the United States 1826 - 1848</u> p. 20

manuscripts of Morgan, with all the printed sheets, were supposed to be in the printing office, it was fired in the night, by a masonic incendiary, with such ingenious preparations as were well calculated to insure its speedy destruction, with that of all its contents . . . The fire was discovered almost as soon as applied, and happily extinguished . . . Other evidences of malice against the printer have been manifested. On one occasion, large numbers of Masonic ruffians, armed with clubs, assembled under different leaders, in the night time, in the vicinity of the printing office, with the declared purpose of obtaining the intended publication, by violence; from which they were prevented only, by the formidable preparations to defend it, made by the printer."[51]

In spite of the opposition of the Freemasons, the book was printed in August of 1826, and sold openly. The book's 96-pages describe the secrets of initiation, passwords, grips, and obligations of the craft. Shortly thereafter, Nicholas Cheseboro, a Freemason from Canandaigua in Ontario County, obtained a warrant for Morgan's arrest over the theft of a shirt and cravat some four months earlier. Cheseboro and several others went to Batavia and arrested Morgan. After stopping at Danold's Tavern, the party then took Morgan to Canandaigua to be tried. Even though charges of theft were quickly thrown out for lack of evidence—Morgan was rearrested, convicted, and jailed for supposedly failing to pay an old debt of $2.69 to one of the town's innkeepers.

---

[51] Demott, B., Freemasonry in American Culture and Society pp. 36 & Morgan, W., Illustrations of Masonry, BY ONE OF THE FRATURNITY, WHO HAS DEVOTED THIRTY YEARS TO THE SUBJECT pp. x - xi, 129, 133 & Vaughn, W., The Anti-Masonic Party in the United States 1826 - 1848 pp. 1 - 4 & The Address of the National Anti-Masonic Convention to the People of the United States p. 4 & Ovason, D., The Secret Architecture of Our Nation's Capital p. 79, 171

The controversy that would surround Morgan's rank revolved around his use of deception and guile to convince the brethren that he was a Royal Arch. Imagine that, Freemasons complaining about pretense! David Miller was an Entered Apprentice Freemason. Finally, the Arch symbolizes the arc of the zodiac.

The Founders' Facade

The next evening, when the jailer was conveniently absent, Cheseboro and some others went to the jail and told the jailer's wife that she could release Morgan into their custody because they had decided to pay his $2.69 debt; reluctantly, she turned the prisoner over to Cheseboro. William Morgan was never seen or heard from again. Vaughn explains:

> *"Morgan was then escorted from the jail. About 9:00 P.M., a shrill whistle sounded, and the jailer's wife rushed to the window, only to see Morgan struggling with two men and shouting 'Murder!' A yellow carriage appeared, and four men threw Morgan into it. The carriage went 'clattering' into the night, and Morgan was never seen in public again . . ."*[52]

The abduction of William Morgan would cause the public to ask many questions. Among them—<u>Were the Freemasons so brazen as to commit murder</u>? And if so, <u>Because so many prominent officials were Freemasons—Would it be possible to bring the culprits to justice if ever captured</u>? Although Freemasons were to block the Morgan investigation in every way they could—through the dogged determination of a few vigilant investigators, coupled with the deathbed testimony of some of those involved—some 69 masons were eventually implicated in the William Morgan kidnapping and murder. The evidence would prove that after taking him from the jail, Morgan was spirited to an abandoned powder magazine at Fort Niagara. After being kept there a week, he was thrown into the Niagara River.

Again, even after the admirable effort and diligence of investigators, the justice system's handling of the proceedings would turn the case into a travesty: though convening 23 grand juries; indicting 54 Freemasons; even bringing 39 to trial—only ten would ever serve any time—and those sentences were only as high as 30-months and as low as 30-days! Later, it was discovered that the judges and many jurors assigned to the case were Freemasons. On top of all of this, many accommodations were made for those who did receive time. For

---

[52] Vaughn, W., <u>The Anti-Masonic Party in the United States 1826 - 1848</u> pp. 4 - 5 & Demott, B., <u>Freemasonry in American Culture and Society</u> p. 37 & Tompkins, P., <u>The Magic of Obelisks</u> p. 316
A cravat can be a scarf worn about the neck or a tie.

example: (1) the convicted parties were allowed to bring personal furnishings to their jail cells; (2) their cell doors were seldom locked; (3) they were permitted to go home on weekends; and (4), one of the Freemasons was even permitted to conduct his daily business affairs from his jail cell.[53]

Though hardly living long enough to see his condemnation of Freemasonry in print—it is rather ironic that Morgan's book should eventually disclose the very way in which the Freemasons would decide his fate and end his life! In an appendix, we are supplied with the eight-page confession of Henry L. Valance. The murderer explained that his declaration was freely given because even after several years—he could not find peace over the role he played in the terrible crime. Here are some excerpts from Valance's confession, in which he speaks of Morgan's condemnation, imprisonment, and death:

> *"He was a thoughtful, silent man, generally, but always ready to act when anything was to be done, and had the reputation among us of being more deeply concerned in the business of kidnapping Morgan than any other of the conspirators. 'Brethren,' he said, in a firm voice, 'there is no denying that our situation is a most critical one; but it is the characteristic of determined, resolute men, that they always rise superior to those difficulties which are fatal to the weak and vacillating. If we are firm, and do not allow ourselves to be deterred from pursuing the only course that can lead to safety, all will yet be well with us. What have we to fear? It is, that Morgan may recover his liberty, and put our order under the ban of public opinion, against which no institution, however strong, can maintain itself. How are these*

---

[53] Bullock, C., <u>Freemasonry and the Transformation of the American Social Order 1730 - 1840</u> pp. 277 - 278 & Vaughn, W., <u>The Anti-Masonic Party in the United States 1826 - 1848</u> pp. 5 - 7 & <u>The Address of the National Anti-Masonic Convention to the People of the United States</u> pp. 5 - 6 & Demott, B., <u>Freemasonry in American Culture and Society</u> p. 37 & <u>Books on Freemasonry: Antimasonic books & pamphlets from the 19th and early 20th century</u> (net) & Morey, R., <u>The Truth About Masons</u> p. 114 & Morgan, W., <u>Illustrations of Masonry, BY ONE OF THE FRATURNITY, WHO HAS DEVOTED THIRTY YEARS TO THE SUBJECT</u> p. 80
Some of the sentencing was as follows: the name of the Freemason who received the 30-month sentence was Eli Bruce; Loton Lawson received 2 years; Nicholas G. Cheesboro received 1 year; John Shelton 3 months; and Edward Sawyer 1 month.

The Founders' Facade

*difficulties to be avoided? To me it seems clear that they can be avoided only by consigning Morgan to that confinement from which alone there is no possible escape—**THAT OF THE GRAVE**! This may appear to some of you a dread alternative, but I have been prepared for it from the beginning as the probable result of this man's seizure and imprisonment . . . Has he not placed himself in the position of a traitor; and have not the laws of God and man, in all ages, condemned traitors to suffer in full the last penalty? <u>And what is the treachery which directs itself only against a country or a king, in comparison with that which aims at the overthrow of a vast institution which is gathering into its folds men of every country, and binding all mankind into a common brotherhood</u>? I say, Morgan has incurred the penalty of death, and that to visit that penalty upon him will be an act of justice . . . Our own safety, too, points to the same course . . ."*

The admission continues:

"We were eight in number, and it was determined that three of us should be selected by lot to perform the part of executioners. Eight pieces of paper were produced, five of which were to remain blank, while the letter D was written on the others. These pieces of paper were placed in a large box, from which each man was to draw one at the same time. After drawing, we all were to separate . . . So soon as we had arrived at certain distances . . . the tickets were to be examined . . . those three who should hold the marked tickets were to proceed to the Fort at midnight, and there put Morgan to death . . ."

I shall end Valance's confession with Morgan's demise at Fort Niagara:

"My comrades left to procure a boat, one of them knowing where it was easy to find it, it having been agreed upon that Morgan should be sunk in the Niagara . . . My part was to proceed to the magazine to prepare him . . . He was pale and haggard, and looked like an old man, though in reality he was not much past the prime of

existence... I was a stranger to him and he hurriedly demanded my business. 'William Morgan,' I replied, 'I come to you on a sad duty—it is to prepare you for your last hour on earth... [Morgan] demanded by what authority we had condemned him? Who had been his judges? were they Americans or foreigners? how was he to die? And many other questions of like character. I told him that I had not come there to answer questions, but to notify him of his sentence... [He] commenced wringing his hands, and talking of his wife and children, the recollection of whom in that awful hour terribly affected him. His wife, he said was young and inexperienced, and his children were but infants... He begged that some permanent provision might be made for them, and, above all things, implored us to communicate his fate to his wife... As we saw no harm in making this promise, which of course we had no idea of keeping, we pledged ourselves to comply with his request, and assured him that his family should not be permitted to suffer from poverty... The time having expired... We each had hold of one of his arms, above the elbow. A short time brought us to where the boat had been placed, and we all entered it... My comrades took the oars, and the boat was rapidly forced out into the river. The night was pitch dark... In the bottom of the boat lay a number of heavy weights, all tied together by a strong cord, that had been carried through the ring of each weight, so that they formed one mass... This cord I took in my hand, and fastened it around the body of Morgan, just above the hips... Then, in a whisper, I bade the unhappy man to stand up, and after a momentary hesitation, he complied with my order. He stood close to the head of the boat, and there was just length enough of rope from his person to the weights to prevent any strain, while he was standing. I then requested one of my associates to assist me in lifting the weights from the bottom to the side of the boat, while the other steadied her from the stern. This was done, and, as Morgan was standing with his back toward me, and apparently looking into the water, I approached him, and gave him a strong push *with both my hands . . . He fell forward, carrying the weights with him, and the waters closed over the mass . . ."*

Little wonder, no single event in the experience of the early nation was to galvanize public opinion against the Freemasons like the kidnapping and murder of William Morgan. After the trial, anti-Masonic conventions were convened across the country—and tens of thousands of Americans would align themselves with the anti-Masonic cause! Meanwhile, hundreds of thousands of copies of Morgan's book were being purchased and studied. It was clear to the American public that Morgan understood his subject matter well, as mere weeks before his murder he would say of Masonry:

> *"Intrenched within these strong walls—decked with all the glitter of high-sounding professions, claiming what does not belong to it,—it dazzles 'but to bewilder and destroy.' In its train, in these United States, are enrolled many periodical works devoted to Masonry; and, under the guise of patronizing mechanics—the arts and sciences lend their aid to carry on the imposing delusion. They take up the specious title of throwing a little illumination on this benighted country, from their secret depositories . . . assuming to be the patron, the life and soul of all that is great and valuable—it deceives many of its votaries . . . Are we astonished at the wild and heedless manner in which many of the votaries of Masonry rush into every excess—putting at defiance the laws of our civil institutions, which suffer no one to be put in jeopardy but by due forms, and disregarding the command of the Most High, which says, thou shalt not kill!—we can readily trace the cause to the impressions and practices obtained from its false tenets and deceptive arrogance."*[54]

---

[54] Morgan, W., <u>Illustrations of Masonry, BY ONE OF THE FRATURNITY, WHO HAS DEVOTED THIRTY YEARS TO THE SUBJECT</u> pp. x, 139 - 145 & Morey, R., <u>The Truth About Masons</u> p. 29 & Vaughn, W., <u>The Anti-Masonic Party in the United States 1826 - 1848</u> pp. 16 - 17, 21 & Tompkins, P., <u>The Magic of Obelisks</u> pp. 318 - 319 & Demott, B., <u>Freemasonry in American Culture and Society</u> pp. 39 - 40

The Crusade Against Freemasonry

In the midst of the Morgan affair, another dilemma for American Freemasonry would begin to take shape; namely, an onslaught by the Christian Church! Briefly, forasmuch as Colonial Masonry was considered a rediscovery of ancient wisdom—religion was not a crucial element of the craft. In fact, a noted historian has observed: *"According to early exposes, Masonic ceremonies of the 1720s seldom included prayers or Bible readings."* Wider acceptance of the Bible in ritual appears to have begun as the colonies approached the Revolutionary War. And by the early 1820s, some were even trying to publicly intertwine Freemasonry with Christianity: hoping that the connection would convey holiness, in the public's eye, and cause Masons to be held above reproach.[55] Of course, as many ministers were aware of the Deism of many of the institution's most prominent figures—from Franklin, to Washington, to Jefferson, to Paine—that would prove no simple task. Yet, with the murder of William Morgan, any artifice to link Freemasonry with Christianity became moot. The blatant disregard for the country's laws and Morgan's life—forced Christian ministers across the land to call for the repudiation of the craft by their membership!

Frankly, one of the greatest combatants against the Freemasons was a former member of the craft. After leaving the institution over the murder of William Morgan—Royal Arch Mason Hiram Hopkins would stir many to take up the anti-Masonic cause! In deference here to Bullock:

> *"Thousands of brothers left the fraternity . . . A shift spurred by Hiram Hopkins's testimony against his former patron and brother, Eli Bruce, in court—and against his fraternity in print. Although Hopkins had once judged Masonry nearly*

---
[55] Bullock, C., <u>Freemasonry and the Transformation of the American Social Order 1730 - 1840</u> pp. 164, 169 - 171

equivalent to Christianity, he now believed almost precisely the opposite. He had been 'trained,' he decided, in the 'school' of Satan."[56]

Against this backdrop, Thurlow Weed would create The Anti-Masonic Enquirer newspaper in 1828. Thurlow focused the paper's efforts on political awareness and the dangers of elitist government within government. About this same time, the Anti-Masonic Party was being formed. Establishing a large Christian and middle class base, by 1829 Thurlow Weed and 20 other A.M.P. candidates would win seats in the New York State legislature. Some of the most notable of the members of the up-start party were John Quincy Adams, Thaddeus Stevens, Milliard Filmore, and William Seward.[57]

The spirit of the A.M.P. platform is summed-up here in a scathing indictment delivered by an A.M.P. delegation at the National Anti-Masonic Convention. This excerpt of The Address of the National Anti-Masonic Convention to the People of the United States of September 11, 1830 declared:

> *"Facts numerous and authentic, demonstrate the existence, in this community, of crimes and dangers, which, upon their first distinct disclosure to honest inquiry, incite equal surprise and solitude; and which can not be reflected upon, by any mind imbued with genuine self-respect, and a just regard for human rights, without the deepest abhorrence and alarm. Freemasonry is the source of these crimes and dangers . . . meetings were attended, and the designs of them approved, by several hundred of the most respectable and intelligent of the masonic brethren. They included legislators, judges, sheriffs, clergymen, generals, physicians, and lawyers."*

---

[56] Bullock, C., Freemasonry and the Transformation of the American Social Order 1730 – 1840 pp. 277 – 278
[57] Demott, B., Freemasonry in American Culture and Society p. 39 & Anti-Masonic Party, The Greenwood Encyclopedia of American Institutions, Political Parties and Civil Action Groups p. 66 & Antimasons, Political Parties and Elections in the United States Vol. I, p. 47 & Richards, L., The Life and Times of Congressman John Quincy Adams pp. 43 – 54 & Tompkins, P., The Magic of Obelisks p. 319 & Books on Freemasonry: Antimasonic books & pamphlets from the 19th and early 20th century (net)

The FreeMasonic Foundations of These United States

The address continued:

> *"Revealed freemasonry is a stupendous mirror, which reflects, in all their horrors, the exact features of that vast spirit of crime, with which this nation is now wrestling, for all that makes life desirable. The grosser parts of this machinery, are secrecy, the private signs, pass words, tokens, grips, and ciphers; the subtler parts are the obligations: and the former are valuable only as they are capable of being employed to give effect to the latter. The obligations . . . compelled such as acknowledged them,—to passive obedience,—to warn each other of all approaching danger,—to conceal each others crimes, even the most aggravated,—to extricate each other from difficulty, right or wrong,—to support each other's reputation in all cases,—to oppose the interest and blast the character of unfaithful brethren,—to sacrifice traitors to freemasonry,—to give each other dishonest preferences,—and to advance each others political preferment in opposition to an other."*[58]

Of course, the Masons vehemently denied these charges. They shot back that these accusations were unjust and that the fraternity was little more than an organization where good and decent men came together in brotherhood. However, a glaring problem with this response and depiction would soon come to the fore. You see, the public was now aware that the craft's secret oaths sanctioned perjury, violence, and sedition![59] For instance, before entering the level of the Royal Arch—a Freemason had to make the following pledge:

> *"I will aid and assist a companion royal arch mason, when engaged in any difficulty, and espouse his cause, so far as to extricate him from the same, if in my*

---

[58] The Address of the National Anti-Masonic Convention to the People of the United States pp. 3 - 4, 11 - 12, 22 - 24
The 111-member delegation was made up mostly of people from the states of New York, Pennsylvania, Massachusetts, and Connecticut.
[59] Higgins, G., Anacalypsis Vol. I, p. 647 & Morey, R., The Truth About Masons p. 112 & UK: The Craft BBC Online Network (net) & Famous Freemasons: Quote by Miguel de Cervantes (net)
The powerful have long held that the best way to keep something secret is to deny its very existence. The fact that Masonic oaths actually call for the murder of those who betray their secrets cannot help but remind us of that celebrated adage: *"Tell me thy company, and I'll tell thee what thou art."*

The Founders' Facade

power, <u>whether he be right or wrong</u> . . . A companion royal arch mason's secrets, given me in charge as such, and I knowing him to be such, shall remain as secure and inviolable, in my breast as in his own, <u>murder and treason not excepted</u> . . ."[60]

The anti-Masonic forces demanded to know why should such a proviso be necessary in an organization whose only purpose was to socialize and perform altruistic acts? Despite the institution's silence, of course, the answer was clear. Before long, the anti-Masonic movement was shaking the nation! Tompkins explains:

> *"Ministers preached the 'satanic nature of the Masonic lodge' and called it incompatible with the Christian faith. Baptists were told to dissolve their ties with Masonry or risk having 'the Hand of Christian Fellowship' withdrawn from them. Other denominations announced they would support no Mason for any office in either town, country, or state. Masons were stricken from jury rolls; and individuals were so persecuted that in many cases they were driven to emigrate. In the early 1830s, of 227 lodges in New York State, only 41 remained. New York's membership dwindled from 20,000 at the time of the Morgan incident to a mere 3,000. All the lodges in Vermont surrendered their charters, and it was the same in all the other states of the Union. As one historian sums it up: The Temple of Masonry was shattered, the brotherhood scattered."*[61]

In 1832, the Anti Masonic Party held a national convention, probably the first of any American party, and nominated William Wirt and Amos Ellmaker to be its candidates for President and Vice President. But as Wirt was a poor campaigner, the ticket was unable to carry the day. Adding insult to injury, Wirt was defeated by incumbent Andrew Jackson who was a known Freemason. A news article of December 5, 1832, reported:

---

[60] <u>The Address of the National Anti-Masonic Convention to the People of the United States</u> p. 9 & <u>Books on Freemasonry: Antimasonic books & pamphlets from the 19th and early 20th century</u> (net)
It is to be noted that this wording was also contained in the oath taken by Master Masons.
[61] Tompkins, P., <u>The Magic of Obelisks</u> pp. 318 - 319

The FreeMasonic Foundations of These United States

"Despite new sectional conflicts, President Jackson was re-elected today, piling up 219 electoral votes to 49 for his chief rival, Henry Clay. Chosen Vice President was Martin Van Burien of New York. Both Jackson and Van Burien are Democrats, while Clay ran on the National Republican ticket. The election marked the first time that the Anti-Masonic Party, which began organizing four years ago, sponsored a candidate, William Wirt, who polled just seven votes. The splinter party opposes the Masonic Order because it considers the order a secret society . . ."[62]

During Jackson's second term a slight air of respectability returned to Freemasonry. Atop this, in the coming years public criticism would begin to mount against the Anti-Masonic Party. Everyone was aware of what the A.M.P. was against—but few candidates were enunciating what they were for. This would lead to the defection of many members of the A.M.P. to the Whig Party. This all notwithstanding, the core of the Anti Masonic Party would not just endure but manage to elect several members to Congress. At their National Convention of 1836, the Party nominated William Harrison to be their second presidential candidate.

In a much better showing than the first race, Harrison would receive 549,508 popular and 73 Electoral votes; but Van Burien was to win the election with 762,978 popular and 170 Electoral votes. After two failed presidential bids, and a decade removed from the Morgan

---

[62] Demott, B., Freemasonry in American Culture and Society p. 39 & Anti-Masonic Party, The Greenwood Encyclopedia of American Institutions, Political Parties and Civil Action Groups p. 66 & Antimasons, Political Parties and Elections in the United States Vol. I, p. 47 & Tompkins, P., The Magic of Obelisks p. 319 & Books on Freemasonry: Antimasonic books & pamphlets from the 19th and early 20th century (net) & James, M., Andrew Jackson: Portrait of A President pp. 246 -247, 307, 310 & Wirt, William, The American Peoples Encyclopedia Vol. XX, p. 172 & Chronicle of America p. 295 & Schleshinger, A., The History of American Presidential Elections 1789 - 1968 Vol. II, p. 574
The figures presented in the article make it appear that public sentiment was overwhelmingly supportive of Jackson; here, once again, the Electoral College would work its magic. In truth, the popular vote for the Presidential Election of 1832 was 687,502 votes for Jackson; the combined totals for Clay and Wirt were 530,189 votes. Yet, these totals are not in any way reflected by the Electoral College tally. Despite receiving more than 40% of the popular vote, the device created a margin of victory for Jackson that was almost four to one.

affair, the membership of the A.M.P. would disband: essentially moving into the Whig and Know Nothing parties. With this, an atmosphere would emerge in which the Freemasons could again openly seek public office. As one author puts it:

> *"There was slight respite when Andrew Jackson, Grand Master of Masons in Tennessee, was elected President for a second term; and then gradually the halls of Masonry once more began to throng with candidates who, after the lesson of Morgan, were more warily chosen from among those whose 'pure lives and characters would make them an ornament to the order.' As the lodges multiplied, Grand Master James Williard was able to announce that thanks to the constancy of members, Freemasonry was once more held in respect and honor in the country . . ."*

With Freemasons being able to openly return to public office—they could once more assert their grip over the government, and see to it that the nation's institutions would serve the interests of the country's elite![63] In truth, the prevailing sentiment of the nation's 19th

---

[63] Demott, B., Freemasonry in American Culture and Society p. 39 & Handlin, O., Daniel Webster and the Rise of Conservatism p. 88 & Antimasons, Political Parties and Elections in the United States Vol. I, p. 47 & Anti-Masonic Party, The Greenwood Encyclopedia of American Institutions, Political Parties and Civil Action Groups p. 67 & Schleshinger, A., The History of American Presidential Elections 1789 - 1968 Vol. II, p. 640 & Chronicle of America p. 304 & Freemasons, Universal Standard Encyclopedia Vol. X, p. 3455 & Tompkins, P., The Magic of Obelisks p. 319 & Books on Freemasonry: Antimasonic books & pamphlets from the 19th and early 20th century (net) & Coleman, J., The Conspirators' Hierarchy: The Committee of 300 pp. 178 - 179

Obviously, Freemasons have not stopped pursuing their aims in this century; indeed, many researchers and ex-Masons have come forward to say as much. For example, Dr. John Coleman's The Conspirators' Hierarchy: The Committee of 300 is a gripping dissertation about the Olympians' designs on world domination. Coleman writes: *"The Committee of 300 consists of certain individuals specialised in their own fields, including cultus diabolicus, mind altering drugs, and specialists in murder by poison, intelligence, banking, and every facet of commercial activity . . . Included in the membership are the old families of the European Black Nobility, the American Eastern Liberal Establishment (in Freemason hierarchy and the Order of Skull and Bones), the Illuminati, or as it is known by the committee 'MORIAH CONQUERING WIND,' the Mumma Group, The National and World Council of Churches, the Circle of Initiates, the Nine Unknown Men, Lucius Trust, Jesuit Liberation Theologists, The Order of the Elders of Zion, the Nasi Princes, International Monetary Fund (IMF), the Bank of International Settlements (BIS) the United Nations, (U.N.), the Central, British Quator Coronati, Italian P2 Masonry-especially those in the Vatican hierarchy-the Central Intelligence Agency, Tavistock Institute selected personnel, various members of leading Foundations and Insurance companies named in the lists that follow, the*

century gentry was that government should only serve the interests of the rich—and the poor should place their hopes in the charity and altruism of the wealthy. In 1890, an article entitled, <u>Top 1 percent owns a monopoly of wealth</u> stated:

> *"Recent estimates suggest more than half the nation's vast new wealth is owned by 1 percent of its population. In 1879, Henry George had already seen the irony in modern economics. 'This association of poverty with progress,' he wrote, 'is the great enigma of our times.' Today, the mystery remains. 'Nature is rich, says George's fellow reformer Henry Demarest Lloyd, 'but everywhere man, the heir of nature, is poor.' Technological progress has allowed man to exploit nature ever more efficiently . . . And cities now confront the existence of a permanent 'dependent class' of wage laborers . . . Most elected officials believe, with Andrew Carnegie, that while unfettered competition in the marketplace 'may be sometimes hard on the individual, it insures the survival of the fittest.'"*[64]

With such sentiment serving as convention, and wealthy Freemasons able to overtly direct the course of the government—hardly surprising that millions of common Americans should come to agree with the earlier assessment by Lincoln that *"Politics, as a trade, finds most and leaves nearly all, dishonest."* Yet and still, while many seek to belittle the efforts of the

---

Hong Kong and Shanghai Bank, the Milner Group-Round Table, Cini Foundation, German Marshall Fund, Ditchley Foundation, Nato, Club of Rome, various environmental groups. The Order of Jerusalem, One World Government Church, Socialist International Black Order, Thule Society, Anenherbe-Rosicrucianists, The Great Superior Ones and literally HUNDREDS of other organisations."

[64] Handlin, O., <u>Daniel Webster and the Rise of Conservatism</u> p. 88 & <u>Chronicle of America</u> p. 484 & Ivins, M., <u>GOP shows little class with class-warfare farce</u> The Seattle Times Jan. 16, 1995 p. B5 & Wallenchinsky, D., & Wallace, I., <u>The Peoples Almanac II</u> p. 310

No less true today than it was in the 1800s, Molly Ivins explains that between 1980 and 1992: *"The pre-tax income of the richest 1 percent of Americans increased by 77 percent (after taxes, 60 per-cent) and that of the top fifth by 29 percent (after taxes, 20 percent). That of the bottom 80 percent of the populace shared 6 percent of the increase in wealth after taxes. Additionally, researchers comment, "Though formally structured as a democratic republic, the U.S. is dominated by an economic and social elite which controls most of the nation's wealth as well as most areas of national and state policy. Because the U.S. allows some class mobility, estimates of the size of the American ruling class vary, but a good figure is about 1/2 of 1% of the population."*

members of the lowly Anti Masonic Party—I believe that they are to be lauded for not only endeavoring to make America live up to the spirit of its creed—but for also understanding that *"none are more hopelessly enslaved than those who falsely believe they are free."*[65]

Albert Pike

Please allow me now to say a word about Albert Pike insomuch as he was a pivotal figure in American Freemasonry. Born in Boston Massachusetts 1809, Pike led a rather undistinguished life until moving to New Orleans and meeting Scottish-Rite Freemason Albert Mackey. Mackey encouraged Pike to become a mason, and in three years, took him from the 4th degree to Grand Commander of the Supreme Council; then came the War Between the States. Though born a Northerner, Pike was a racist who fought for the South in the Civil War. In the words of Pike:

---

[65] Jameson, W., Return of Assassin John Wilkes Booth p. 8 & Know-Nothing Movement, Encyclopedia Americana Vol. XVI, p. 520 & Know-Nothing Party, The American Peoples Encyclopedia Vol. XI, p. 983 & Booth, John Wilkes, Dictionary of American Biography Vol. I, p. 449 & Douglas, C., Forty Thousand Quotations p. 1328 & Seldes, G., The Great Quotations p. 866 & Preuss, A., Dictionary of Secret and Other Societies p. 326 & Morey, R., The Truth About Masons pp. 109 - 110 & Beauregard, E., Edwin M. Stanton and Freemasonry Lincoln Herald Vol. 95, No. 4 1993 p. 124 - 126 & The Crown and the Capitol - Abraham Lincoln (net) & Beauregard, E., The Chief Prosecutor of Andrew Johnson Midwest Quarterly Vol. 31, No. 4 1990 pp. 408 - 422

Having quoted Lincoln, I might add here that as a member of the Virginia Militia and The Supreme Order of the Star Spangled Banner (its supporters called "Know Nothings" because of the blanket of secrecy they maintained about the Order) John Wilkes Booth, like Edwin M. Stanton and Andrew Johnson, was no stranger to Freemasonry. Indeed, it is widely reported that Booth was an acquaintance of Vice President Andrew Johnson. While many eerie parallels have been drawn between the Presidents Lincoln and Kennedy, and their predecessors Andrew Johnson and Lyndon Johnson—it is also to be noted that these Presidents' stated assassins both had the same number of letters in their names: fifteen. The other comment was made by Johann Wolfgang von Goethe. Incidentally, the Catholics would continue their ban on Freemasonry. The Orthodox Presbyterian Church was to denounce Freemasonry for its anti-Christian tenants in 1942. The Lutherans would also ban masons from their congregations in 1964. Actually, even as late as 1974, we find the Christian Reformed Church denouncing Freemasonry as being a religion unto itself.

The FreeMasonic Foundations of These United States

"I took my obligation to White men, not to Negroes. When I have to accept Negroes as brethren or leave freemasonry, I shall leave it!"

With the South's defeat, Albert Pike fled to Canada. With the assassination of Lincoln, President Andrew Johnson (who also was a Freemason) granted the Grand Commander of the Supreme Council amnesty for his wartime activities. It was this period, during the nation's reorganizational years after the war, that former Confederate General and Freemason Nathan Bedford Forrest founded the Ku Klux Klan. Albert Pike was the Ku Klux Klan's first Chief Justice, and it is widely held that he was the creator of its early rites. During these years, Albert Pike would be acknowledged as America's most influential Freemason.

Through the years, Pike would create the Order's instructions for the operations of its 4th through 33rd degrees. Historians explain that Pike was greatly influenced by the anti-Christian brand of Freemasonry that was practiced by the French, especially that of the notorious French Magician and Occultist Alphonse Louis Constant. Also known as Eliphas Levi Zahed, Constant is well known for his admiration and efforts to conjure demons and magical angels! Also becoming a devotee of the Vedas (scriptures of the Hindus), Pike is said to have deemed the Masonic Triangle to represent Krishna, Shiva, and Brahma. What's more, Pike would not merely come to see Freemasonry as a religion—<u>he would declare the Hindu faith to be man's oldest religion and Christianity to be evil</u>! Of Pike's influence on Scottish-Rite Freemasonry, Morey writes: *"Pike attempted to remold Scottish freemasonry into an Aryan religion for the Aryan race complete with its own scriptures, ceremonies and symbolism. He was deeply involved in occult arts such as magic and astrology as well . . ."*

The Grand Master Freemason Albert Pike died on April 2, 1891. Incredibly, despite originally being buried in the Oak Hill Cemetery on April 16, 1891—by a special act of the Congress of the United States in 1944—Albert Pike was exhumed and re-interred in the

The Founders' Facade

House of the Temple in Washington D.C. (Headquarters of Scottish-Rite Freemasonry in the United States). Incidentally, J. Edgar Hoover was another Freemason who was afforded unusual burial privileges by the government.[66]

In closing, since a great many things, pro and con, have been written about Pike's influence upon Scottish-Rite Freemasonry, permit me to leave you with a few passages from his work, Morals and Dogma of the Ancient and Accepted Scottish Rite of Freemasonry, so that you might be able to form some of your own opinions:

On page 277 we read:

> "*The first Masonic Legislator whose memory is preserved to us by history, was Bouddh, who, reformed the religion of Manous.*"

On page 11 we find:

---

[66] Morey, R., The Truth About Masons pp. 35 - 56 & Whalen, W., Christianity and American Freemasonry p. 21 & Freemasonry Watch: - It was Johnson (net) & The KKK and the KOL, "Masonic" brotherhoods which suppressed reforms (net) & Eliphas Lévi: The Man Behind Baphomet (net & Colossians 2: 18 & Higgins, G., Anacalypsis p. 105 & Seldes, G., The Great Quotations p. 57 & Demott, B., Freemasonry in American Culture and Society pp. 102 - 103, 149 - 151 & Quarles, B., The Negro in the American Revolution & Preuss, A., Dictionary of Secret and Other Societies pp. 140 - 144, 324 - 326 & Aptheker, H., American Negro Slave Revolts p. 50 & Bullock, C., Freemasonry and the Transformation of the American Social Order 1730 - 1840 pp. 158 - 162 & Freemasons, Universal Standard Encyclopedia Vol. X, p. 3454 & (Video), Frontline: The Secret File on J. Edgar Hoover 1993 & Grimshaw, W., Official History of Freemasonry Among Colored People in North America

Permit me to share this brief assessment of the notion of Aryan superiority by the German philosopher Friedrich Nietzsche: "*The Aryan influence perverted the whole world . . . Mixed races are the sources of great civilizations . . . Never speak to a man who believes in the race fraud.*" Centuries before the life of Pike, the Apostle Paul would warn: "*Do not let anyone who delights in false humility and the worship of angels disqualify you for the prize. Such a person goes into great detail about what he has seen, and his unspiritual mind puffs him up with idle notions.*" Finally, just so there will be no confusion, Blacks have practiced Freemasonry in America since 1775. Prince Hall of Boston is widely considered to be the first prominent Black Mason in America. Yet, make no mistake about it—considered "*spurious*" by White Masons—the Black craft was not connected with White American Orders in any way. In fact, as late as the 1950s, scholars would explain: "*There is no affiliation between white and Negro Freemasonry in the United States . . .*"

The FreeMasonic Foundations of These United States

"The 'Holy Bible, Square, and Compass,' are not only styled the Great Lights in Masonry, but they are also technically called the 'Furniture' of the Lodge; and, as you have seen, it is held that there is no lodge without them. This has sometimes been made a pretext for excluding Jews from our Lodges . . . The Bible is an indispensable part of the 'furniture' of a Christian Lodge, only because it is the sacred book of the Christian religion. The Hebrew Pentateuch in a Hebrew Lodge, and the Koran in a Mohammedan one, belong to the Altar; and one of these, and the Square and Compass, properly understood, are the Great lights by which a Mason must walk. The obligation of the candidate is always to be taken on the sacred book or books of his religion, that he may deem it more solemn and binding; and therefore it was that you were asked of what religion you were. We have no other concern with your religious creed."

On page 295 and 296, Pike writes:

"The God of nineteen-twentieths of the Christian world is only Bel, Moloch, Zeus, or at best Osiris, Mithras, or Adonai, under another name, worshipped with the old pagan ceremonies and ritualistic formulas."

On page 212 and 213:

"Books, to be of religious tendency in the Masonic sense, need not be books of sermons, of pious exercises, or of prayers. Whatever inculcates pure, noble, and patriotic sentiments, or touches the heart with the beauty of virtue, and excellence of an up-right life, accords with religion of Masonry, and is the Gospel of literature and art. That Gospel is preached from many a book and painting . . . Every Masonic Lodge is a temple of religion; and its teachings are instruction in religion. For here are inculcated disinterestedness, affection, toleration, devotedness, patriotism, truth, generous sympathy with those that suffer and mourn, pity for the fallen, mercy for the erring, relief for those in want, Faith, Hope, and Charity. Here

The Founders' Facade

we meet as brethren, to learn how to know and love each other."

On page 321 Pike says:

"The Apocalypse is, to those who receive the nineteenth degree, the Apotheosis of that Sublime Faith which aspires to God alone, and despises all the pomps and works of Lucifer. Lucifer, the 'Light-bearer!' Strange and mysterious name to give to the Spirit of Darkness! Lucifer, the Son of the Morning! Is it 'he' who bears the 'Light,' and with its splendors intolerable blinds feeble, sensual, or selfish souls! Doubt it not! for traditions are full of Divine Relations and Inspirations: and Inspiration is not of one Age or of one Creed . . ."

Finally, on page 860 and 861 we read:

"The force that repels a Planet from the Sun is no more an 'evil' force, than that which attracts the Planet toward the central Luminary; for each is created and exerted by the Deity. And the result is the harmonious movement of the obedient Planets . . . Of that Equilibrium, possible in ourselves, and Masonry incessantly labors to accomplish in its Initiates, and demands of its Adepts and Princes (else unworthy of their titles), between the Spiritual and Divine and the Material and human in man; between the intellect, Reason, and Moral Sense on one side, and the Appetites and Passions on the other, from which result the Harmony and Beauty of a well-regulated life. Which possible Equilibrium proves to us that our Appetites and Senses are also Forces given unto us by God, for purposes of good, and not the fruits of the malignancy of a Devil, to be detested, mortified, and, if possible, rendered inert and dead . . . And this Equilibrium teaches us, above all, to reverence ourselves as immortal souls, and to have respect and charity for others, who are even such as we are, partakers with us of the Divine Nature, lighted by a ray of the Divine Intelligence, struggling like us, toward the light . . . From the mutual action and re-action of each of these pairs of opposites and contraries results that which

with them forms the Triangle, to all the Ancient Sages the expressive symbol of the Deity; as from Osiris and Isis, Har-oeri, the Master of Light, and Life, and the Creative Word. At the angles of one stand, symbolically, the three columns that support the Lodge, itself a symbol of the Universe, Wisdom, Power, and Harmony or Beauty . . . And as in each Triangle of Perfection, one is three and three are one, so man is one, though of a double nature; and he attains the purposes of his being only when the two natures that are in him are in just equilibrium . . . Such . . . is the True Word of a Mason; such the true ROYAL SECRET, which makes possible, and shall at lengths make real, the HOLY EMPIRE of true Masonic Brotherhood."

The Plot to Seize America

Moving into the 20th century, we find little changing within the corridors of power. Despite all the public denials of the behind the scenes dealings of the wealthy and powerful—by the 1930's, the true disposition of the nation's upper crust would once more be made clear for the world to see. In 1934, a fascist conspiracy to overthrow the U.S. Government, backed by wealthy American financiers, would come to light! This overthrow of the United States government was supposed to be led by General Smedley Butler, and a military contingent of some 500,000 veterans. In truth, the reason that the plan was not carried out was due in large part to the unanticipated patriotism of General Butler himself!

Archer explains that sworn testimony given in secret executive hearings before the Committee on Un-American Activities, would implicate members of the Rockefeller, Mellon, Pew, Pitcarin, and Hutton families—and such business concerns as Morgan, Dupont, Remington, Anaconda, Bethlehem, Goodyear, G.M.C., Swift, and Sun. All of these players were participants in the plot to topple the government and seize the nation by force!

The Founders' Facade

Apparently, <u>nothing short of fascism would ensure freedom</u> in their estimation. According to Seldes:

> *"General Smedley Butler testified before a Congressional Committee that several Wall Street bankers, one of them connected with J.P. Morgan & Co., several founders of the American Liberty League, and several heads of the American Legion plotted to seize the government of the United States shortly after President Roosevelt established the New Deal. The press, with a few exceptions, suppressed the news. Worse yet, the McCormick-Dickstein Committee suppressed the facts involving the big business interests, although it confirmed the plot which newspapers and magazines had either refused to mention or had tried to kill by ridicule."*

The failure of the American Press notwithstanding—an excerpt of Report 153 of the 1st session of the 74th Congress (pursuant to House Resolution No. 198, 73d Congress) was to state the following about this conspiracy: *"There is no question that these attempts were discussed, were planned, and might have been placed in execution when and if the financial backers deemed it expedient."* It is to be noted here that many of the conspiracy's wealthy ringleaders had originally wanted either General Douglass MacArthur or Hanford MacNider, both high ranking Freemasons, to lead the military takeover—but were forced to enlist General Butler because MacArthur and Hanford were held in contempt by many veterans for their opposition to bonus pay for WWI veterans. But had veteran sentiment about MacArthur or MacNider been different, and had the financiers chosen either of them to carryout the overthrow of the government in 1934—Who Knows . . .[67]

---

[67] The Plot to Seize the White House (review by Dale Wharton) (net) & Seldes, G., One Thousand Americans pp. 287 - 298 & Seldes, G., The Great Quotations p. 766 & Spivak, J., A Man in His Time pp. 294 - 331 & (Video), History's Mysteries: The Plot to Overthrow F.D.R. 1999 & Friend To Friend (net) & MacNider, H., The National Cyclopedia of American Biography Vol. 54, pp. 2 - 3

Seldes' assessment lends credence to Einstein's observation: *"The (American) press, which is mostly controlled by vested interests, has an excessive influence on public opinion."* Report 153 was released February 15, 1935. Obviously, the political assassinations and cover-ups of the 1960s, leave no doubt that the aims of those who have ubiquitously come to be known as <u>They</u> would not change . . .

Masonic Symbolism

Questions of loyalty to the Constitution and social benevolence notwithstanding, allow me to close with a few illustrations of the integration of Masonic symbolism and culture into the matrix of the nation. Let's begin with the Great Seal of the United States. The emblem's chief designer, Charles Thomson, was Secretary of the Continental Congress and a member of Benjamin Franklin's American Philosophical Society. While there is debate as to whether Thomson was a formal Freemason—there can be no doubt that the design he would ultimately commission to represent the country is filled with Masonic symbolism.

The Founders' Facade

The 32 feathers in the right wing and 33 feathers of the left wing of the American eagle represent degrees in Scottish-Rite Freemasonry; the 9 tail feathers represents the degrees in the York Rite; the Latin phrase *E Pluribus Unum* ("From Many comes One") is an allusion to the Masonic brotherhood; the 13 stars above the eagle are clustered so as to form the six-pointed Star of David (reminding masons of David's dream of the temple that Solomon would later build); and, the unfinished 13 course pyramid beneath the All-Seeing Eye imparts the immortality of the soul to masons.

Seal of the United States

The FreeMasonic Foundations of These United States

Seal of the United States

In actual point of fact, the number thirteen is displayed quite often in the Masonic symbolism of the founders: there are 13 red and white stripes on the nation's flag; there were 13 original colonies; on the back of the one-dollar bill there are 13 levels in the Pyramid (incidentally, this also happens to be the emblem of the Illuminati of Bavaria); the words *Annuit Coeptis* over the pyramid have 13 letters; and, according to Goodman—the Latin word *Saeclorum* was intentionally spelled wrong to create 39 (or 3 x 13) characters within the circle of the seal. On the reverse side we find: 13 bars in the banner shield of the eagle; the eagle has 13 arrows in its right claw and 13 olive leaves in it's left claw; there are 13 stars above the eagle's head; and, there are 13 letters in *E Pluribus Unum* on the ribbon clenched

The Founders' Facade

in the eagle's jaw. Now, the number thirteen and a snake (ribbon) in the beak of a bird have long held mystic implications. Furthermore, the first bird chosen for the nation's seal was not the bald eagle, but the phoenix—the most sacred bird of the ancient Egyptians (please see Chapter Notes). Atop all this, the point has also been made that by inverting the pyramid in the country's seal to create a six-pointed star, the letters s, m, o, n and a are indicated, which can be rearranged to form the word Mason.

To continue on, the nation's Freemasons have also utilized geometry to convey their messages. If the truth is to be told, geometry is considered to be one of the pillars of Freemasonry. Morgan would disclose the following:

"The study of the liberal arts, that valuable branch of education, which tends so effectually to polish and adorn the mind, is earnestly recommended to your consideration; especially the science of Geometry, which is established as the basis of our art. Geometry, or Masonry, originally synonymous terms, being of a divine moral nature, is enriched with the most useful knowledge . . ."

Remarkably, the geometric and architectural layout of Washington D.C. is also a clear expression of Freemasonry. In Ovason's, The Secret Architecture of Our Nation's Capital: The Masons and the Building of Washington D.C. we find:

"'As above, so below.' These words, attributed to [ancient Africa's] Hermes Trismegistus, lie at the heart of Western esoteric tradition. In brief, they mean that the universe and all it contains is reflected in some manner not only on earth, but also in man and his works . . . Not only have the stars guided the traveler on earth and the seas, but their constellations are archetypes that have been viewed as guides for the lives of men and nations."

The author also states: *"Underlying the Masonic symbolism of initiation is a profound grasp of the cosmic bodies which are the subject of astrology."* Ovason goes on to painstakingly demonstrate that dozens of monuments and buildings were erected and commemorated in Washington D.C., in relation to the constellations—especially the sign Virgo. A member of the Cincinnati, Pierre Charles L' Enfant, who was commissioned by George Washington to layout the new federal city, would establish a triangular design of cardinal buildings that would correspond to the constellation of Virgo within the first magnitude stars Regulus, Arcturus, and Spica: Regulus, or little ruler, represents the Capitol (whose cornerstone was laid when the Dragon's head was in Virgo); Arcturus, or the watcher, represents the White House (whose cornerstone was laid when the Dragon's head was in Virgo); and finally Spica, or power and glory, represents the land's Washington Monument (whose foundation stone was also laid when the Dragon's head was in Virgo).

It is rather interesting that the cornerstones of America's cardinal buildings, her foremost and oldest stately treasures if you will, should be laid when the Dragon's head was in the house of Virgo—the sign of the Virgin. While some will try to associate such Virgoan principles as chastity, reliability, and stability with the Dragon—and then, somehow, on to these buildings—I must reject that! In fact, I deem it oxymoronic on its face: a bit like choosing a turtle to symbolize the world's fastest sprinter! Perhaps, <u>the actual meaning of the position of the Dragon's head is not to convey respect for the celestial Virgin, but rather, her destruction—and that of her offspring! Indeed, William Morgan declared as much; a disclosure, bye the way, that may well have been the very reason the Masons murdered him.</u>

No less illuminating here, those of you who are Christians must recall the passage in Revelations, which speaks of the wondrous woman and the great red Dragon:

> *"Now a great sign appeared in heaven: a woman clothed with the sun, and the moon under her feet, and upon her head a crown of twelve stars: And she being with child cried, travailing in birth, and pained to be delivered. And there appeared another wonder in heaven; and behold a great red dragon, having seven heads and ten horns, and seven crowns upon his heads. And his tail drew the third part of the*

stars of heaven, and did cast them to the earth; and the dragon stood before the woman which was ready to be delivered, for to devour her child as soon as it was born . . ."

Since most today will scoff at, and summarily reject, the idea that these revolutionary Deists might actually dare to establish a nation that was anti-religious—even though Walters would describe the founding fathers as, "<u>opposed uncompromisingly, to supernaturalist religions in general and Christianity in particular</u>"—I guess we must characterize the fact that the Dragon's head was in Virgo for the laying of the cornerstones of the Capitol, White House, and Washington Monument as happenstance: nothing but sheer coincidence. In passing however, a century and a half later, Brigadier General Brehon Somervell would determine that the construction of the Pentagon should commence on September 11, 1941; oh' yeah, you guessed it—when the Dragon's head once more just happened to be in the house of Virgo. Lastly here, the dragon is mentioned 13 times in the New Testament—and there is not one instance when it is depicted as an agent for righteousness . . .

The Symbol of Baphomet

Baphomet (the Goat Head) is represented by an upside-down five-pointed star

Credible researchers have even demonstrated that the White House is geometrically positioned so as to represent the base of an upside-down pentagram (five-pointed star). It has to be said that this symbol has long been considered as the symbol of Baphomet in Freemasonry.[i]

The FreeMasonic Foundations of These United States

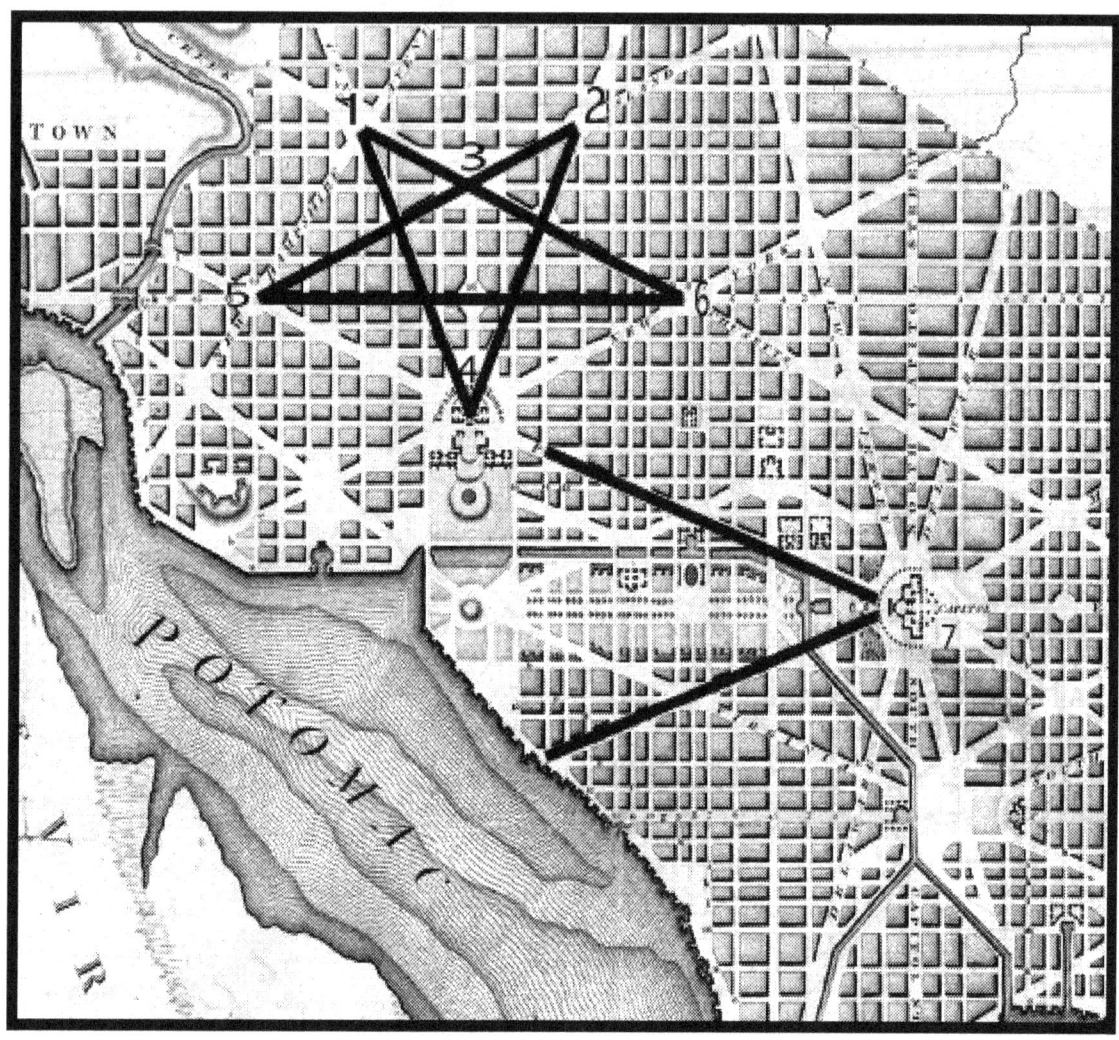

Official Plan of the City of Washington - 1800
1 Dupont Circle, 2 Logan Circle, 3 Scott Circle, 4 White House, 5 Washington Circle, 6 Mt Vernon Square, 7 The Capitol

As one researcher would put it:

> "*Our Founding Fathers who were Freemasons, intended from the beginning, that Washington, D.C., Government Center, was to be established as a Freemason Capitol. They intended that Freemasons would determine the political and spiritual direction of the infant United States of America . . . This fulfills the stated objective of Albert Pike in his book, <u>Morals and Dogma</u>, hiding the truth from the 'Profane' while*

revealing it to the 'Elect' . . . the true center of spiritual and political power resides only in the Freemason Temple of Understanding, located 13 blocks north of the White House, and directly in line with the massive obelisk known as the Washington Monument. Occultists believe that the spirit of the Sun God 'Ra' indwells the obelisk, and that the 'Elect' must bow down before it twice to three times daily. Thus, the Washington Monument, the obelisk, is in direct line [on the square] with the Congress to its East, and with the Freemason Temple directly North. The White House is not in direct line with the obelisk, which is very revealing as to the planned center of power . . ."[69]

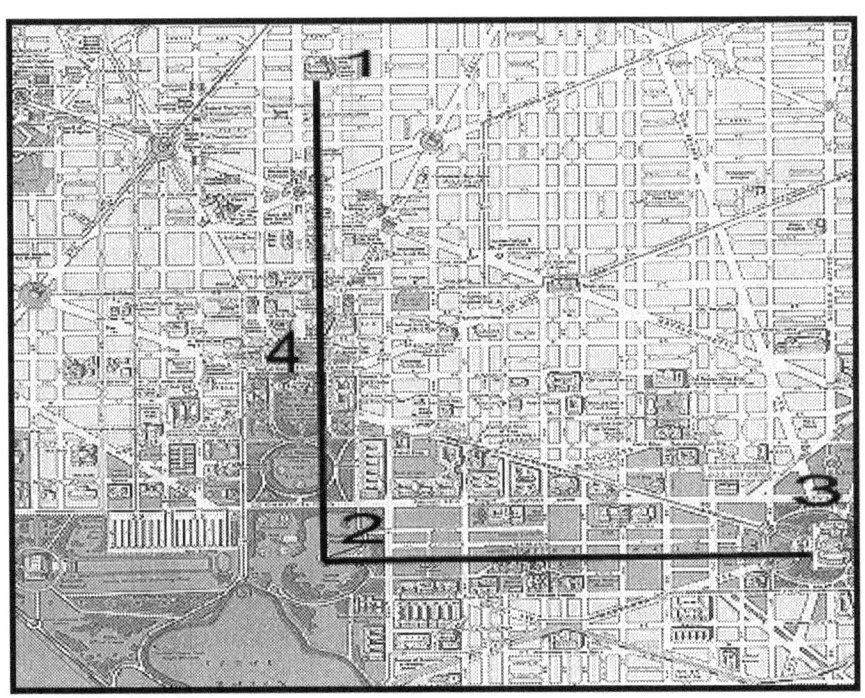

1 House of the Temple, 2 Washington Monument, 3 Capitol, 4 White House

---

[69] <u>Freemasonry Source Confirms our Article: Masonic Symbols of Power in Their Seat of Power</u> (net) & Morey, R., <u>The Truth About Masons</u> pp. 35 - 56 & & Goodman, F., <u>Magic Symbols</u> pp. 136 -137 & Demott, B., <u>Freemasonry in American Culture and Society</u> pp. 102 - 103, 149 - 151 & Preuss, A., <u>Dictionary of Secret and Other Societies</u> pp. 140 - 144, 324 - 326 & Bullock, C., <u>Freemasonry and the Transformation of the American Social Order 1730 - 1840</u> pp. 158 - 162 & Ovason, D., <u>The Secret Architecture of Our Nation's Capital</u> pp. 244 - 245, 366 - 367 & Walters, K., <u>Rational Infidels: The American Deists</u> p. 39 & <u>Esso pictorial guide to Washington, D.C., and vicinity : 1942</u>

A similar architectural observation is to be made of Paris; indeed, there is a strikingly unobstructed view from the entrance of the Pantheon (the resting place of several of France's greatest Freemasons) and the Eiffel Tower.

Adams & Kennedy

It is blatantly clear that bravery and principle are traits seldom found in American politics: indeed, all of the national movements that would lead to the uplifting of the majority of its citizens, first requiring Herculean struggle from men and women outside of the political arena—with the politicians eventually being dragged along kicking and screaming. However, two American presidents would possess the fortitude to publicly oppose the institution of Freemasonry: John Quincy Adams and John Fitzgerald Kennedy.

As to the former, in an address to the People of Massachusetts, John Quincy Adams would remark: *"I saw a code of Masonic legislation adapted to prostrate every principle of equal justice and to corrupt every sentiment of virtuous feeling in the soul of him who bound his allegiance to it."* Adams was to continue:

> *"I saw the practice of common honesty, the kindness of Christian benevolence, even the abstinence of atrocious crimes; limited exclusively by lawless oaths and barbarous penalties, to the social relations between the Brotherhood and the Craft. I saw slander organize into a secret, widespread and affiliated agency . . . I saw self-invoked imprecations of throats cut from ear to ear, of hearts and vitals torn out and cast off and hung on spires. I saw wine drunk from a human skull with solemn invocation of all the sins of its owner upon the head of him who drank it."*

As to the latter, on April 27, 1961, President Kennedy would state the following in an Address to the nation's newspaper publishers:

> *"The very word "secrecy" is repugnant in a free and open society; and we are as a people inherently and historically opposed to secret societies, to secret oaths and to*

secret proceedings. We decided long ago that the dangers of excessive and unwarranted concealment of pertinent facts far outweighed the dangers, which are cited to justify it."

Permit me to conclude this inquiry into the Freemasonic foundations of these United States with this brief passage from Steven Bullock's <u>Freemasonry and the Transformation of the American Social Order 1730 – 1840</u>:

> *"On September 18, 1793, President George Washington dedicated the United States Capitol. Dressed in Masonic Apron, the president placed a silver plate upon the cornerstone and covered it with the Masonic symbols of corn, oil, and wine. After a prayer, the brethren performed 'chanting honors.' Volleys of artillery punctuated the address that followed. Like the entire ceremony, the silver plate identified Freemasonry with the Republic; it was laid, it stated, 'in the thirteenth year of American independence . . ."*[70]

The Capitol and the Washington Monument

---

[70] <u>Freemasonry Watch: The First Degree of Freemasonry Watch</u> (net) & Bullock, C., <u>Freemasonry and the Transformation of the American Social Order 1730 – 1840</u> p. 137

The FreeMasonic Foundations of These United States - Chapter Notes

[i] Schmidt, A., Fraternal Organizations pp. 121 - 122 & Hall, M., The Secret Teachings of All Ages pp. LXXVII - LXXVIII & pp. 42 - 49 & Percival, H., Masonry and its Symbols pp. 42 - 49 & Thirteen, Man, Myth, and Magic Vol. XIX, pp. 2606 - 2607 & Freemasons (net) & American Freemasonry: A Delusional Cultural Foundation for Repressive Social Control (net) & (Video), The World's Greatest Conspiracies 1997 & (Video), Transformation of Myth Through Time: From the Id to the Igo in the Orient W. Free 1989 & Morgan, W., Illustrations of Masonry, BY ONE OF THE FRATURNITY, WHO HAS DEVOTED THIRTY YEARS TO THE SUBJECT p. Intro., 48 & Ovason, D., The Secret Architecture of Our Nation's Capital p. vii, 45, 75, 103, Chap. 4, 9 & Revelations Chap. 12 & Astrology: Dragons throughout the ages - Dragons importance in Astrology (net) & Did You Know? Under the pressure of war, the Corps built the Pentagon in 16 months? (net) & Freemasonry and Washington D.C.'s Street Layout (net) & Goodman, F., Magic Symbols pp. 10 - 11, 17, 73 - 76, 80 - 99, 109 - 112, 114, 140 - 141 & Pike, A., Morals and Dogma of the Ancient and Accepted Scottish Rite of Freemasonry pp. 15, 465 - 468 & Levi, E., Dogma Et Rituel de la Haute Magie pp. 56, 121 & Albert Pike, Mystic Pt 1 (net) & Famous Freemasons: Quote by Cervantes (net)

In European magical belief, thirteen is the number of necromancy (temporarily bringing the dead back to life). In the Tarot tradition thirteen is the number of death. Thirteen is also the number of a coven of witches: twelve witches and the devil. The proper spellings would be *saeclorum* or *saeculorum;* however, neither of these would produce a total of 39 letters and numbers in the circle of the seal. It is also to be noted that Joseph Campbell makes associations between the eye of the pyramid on the dollar bill and the Hindu religion. In addition, Goodman explains the following: *"In fact, the shape recalls the Egyptian hieroglyphic () called the 'Ru', which is at once a symbol of a doorway and of the female sexual organs: it is sometimes called the 'gate of birth'. The idea is that through this shape a spiritual form or light shines out into the material world, and that through this doorway spiritual beings pass."* He goes on, *"The occultist Madame Blavatsky records some interesting occult symbols which have been derived from this Ru form . . . including the symbol which represents the 'Third Eye' of popular occultism. She claims also that the form called the 'pasa', which is held in the hands of the Hindu god Siva, is derived from the Ru . . . The Medieval artist constructed a shape similar to the Ru in order to convey the idea of 'spiritual birth' or of a 'doorway into spirit', basing their figure on geometric principles which were mystical or magical."* The truth is that the first bird chosen to represent the nation was not the bald eagle, but the phoenix of ancient Egyptian lore! On page XC of his AN ENCYCLOPEDIC OCTLINE OF Masonic, Hermetic, Qabbalistic and Rosicrucian Symbolical Philosophy, Albert Mackey states: "European mysticism was not dead at the time the United States was founded. The hand of the Mysteries controlled in the establishment of the new government, for the signature of the Mysteries may still be seen on the Great Seal of the United States *of America. Careful analysis of the seal discloses a mass of occult and Masonic symbols, chief among them the so-called American eagle—a bird Benjamin Franklin declared unworthy to be chosen as the emblem of a great, powerful, and progressive people. Here again only the student of symbolism can see through the subterfuge and realize that the American eagle upon the Great Seal is but a conventionalized phoenix, a fact plainly discernible from an examination of the original seal . . . In an colored sketch submitted by William Baton in 1782, an actual phoenix appears sitting upon a nest of flames . . ."* In the Royal Arch Degrees the six-pointed star symbolizes power and intelligence. This Star of David is also known as the Seal of Solomon. Daring to consider the Dragon's head in the house of the Virgin for a malevolent rather than benevolent purpose—might help us to understand the early nation's view of women in general—and the treatment of the Black woman in particular. Indeed, women in ancient Egypt possessed more societal rights than women in early America! Through the ages, upright five-pointed have been symbols for Sirius, Horus, and Thoth. However, it appears that the up-right five-pointed star can represent unity, or the keys of heaven, earth, and hell in contemporary Freemasonry. The six geographic locations that represent the points of the goat head are Dupont Circle, Logan Circle, Scott Circle, Washington Circle, Mt. Vernon Square, and the White House. FYI: in mystic symbolism, the circle is said to impart spiritual force—and the four corners of a square represent the spirit enmeshed in time. Indeed, an Irish poem recited by 19th century Masons goes: *"I will strive to live - With love & care - Upon the level - By the square."* One other point here is that a pentagon can clearly be seen within the center of the star of Baphomet (see page 89). Of course, many of you are saying, *"Devils...Smevils...who has time for that?"* Well, one person who made time for it was the French Magician and Occultist Alphonse Louis Constant. Also known as Eliphas Levi Zahed, Constant was noted for his involvement with necromancy (the effort to conjure dead people, demons, or magical angels to reveal the future and influence events). In his <u>Dogma Et Rituel de la Haute Magie</u>, Levi wrote: *"In the occult sciences all is real, and theories are established only on the foundations of experience. Realities alone constitute the proportions of the ideal, and the Magus admits nothing as certain in the domain of ideas save that which is demonstrated by realization. In other words, what is true in the cause manifests in the effect. What is not realized does not exist . . ."* He also stated: *"Professions of faith are formulations of the ignorance and aspirations of man. The theorems of science are monuments of his conquests. The man who denies God is no less fanatical than he who defines Him with pretended infallibility. God is commonly defined by the enumeration of all that He is not . . . Man can realize that which he believes in the measure of that which he knows, by reason of that which he knows not, and he can accomplish all that he wills in the measure of that which he believes and by reason of that which he knows."* As mentioned, Levi is known to have had a profound influence upon Albert Pike! What was that heralded Moorish saying—Oh' yeah—*"Tell me thy company, and I'll tell thee what thou art."* Finally here, a little food for thought: If some group was to commit themselves to a philosophy in which, systematic lies and deception were acceptable practices—and material gain and world domination were to be sought at all cost—what could be a better name for the seat of their benightedness, than "The White House?"

Epilogue

The Founders' Facade

The founders of America understood that since no man has any natural authority over another, and force is no warranty of righteousness—social convention was their government's best hope for acceptance. Hence, the need for the formation of such widely held Western attitudes as—*Ignorance is bliss*; *It is the duty of the old to lie to the young*; *The evil we do today is for the greater good of tomorrow*; *Insomuch as the rich are always right, it only follows that poor are always wrong*; and, *Yours' is not to reason why, Yours' is but to do and die*. However, let's be clear—these positions were not popularized for the sake of the nation's numeric majority—but by, and for, its wealthy minority.

That said, and despite having made these troubling disclosures about the nation and its founders—far be it from me to tell anyone how to live his or her life. First, no one knows your talents and aspirations better than you. Secondly, the pools that feed the streams of your passions must spring from within. Yet, please permit me this one indulgence: If the pools which feed the streams of your passions be false—whether conventional or not—the reservoir of your zeal for life will become the quicksand of your death.

So, as you journey through life, whenever you are in doubt—seek the truth! I can't help be reminded of the ancient Egyptian maxim: *"Truth can make a way, even for the ignorant!"* No less important, once you begin to see the reality, never permit the chasm that exists between it and the façade unhinge you from the moral compass. Choosing to follow the truth—though not easy—will bring greater understanding, self-actualization, and a self-determination that will culminate in the attainment of heights never before imagined! On the other hand, those who continue to embrace the façade can expect even greater diminishing returns from more of the same . . .

In closing, despite the fact that many wholeheartedly embrace the latter—**I Celebrate Your Selection Of The Former** because it is a requisite of our adulthood that we shun lies! Be well told, however, it is a choice that may very well require you to stand-alone at times. Indeed, no less a figure than Albert Einstein would explain that people who embrace the truth have always encountered opposition from those who do not. But take heart; and through it all, please never forget: In a great house there are many vessels—some of gold, and some of silver, some of wood, and some of earth—that which is to be honored in time, and that which is not! A brave soul once said, *It is not a character flaw to make a mistake; the flaw lies in failing to attempt a correction once you become aware of it!*

Bibliography

The Founders' Facade

Altman, S., The Encyclopedia of African-American Heritage Facts on File 1997

Aptheker, H., American Negro Slave Revolts International Publ. 1943

Augarde, T., The Oxford Dictionary of Modern Quotations Oxford 1991

Barker, C., American Convictions: Cycles of Public Thought 1600 - 1850 Lippincott 1970

Barry, J., Masonry and the Flag Masonic Serv. Assn. 1924

Bartlett, J., Familiar Quotations: A Collection of Passages, Phrases, and Proverbs Traced to Their Ancient and Modern Sources Little, Brown 1992

Beauregard, E., Edwin M. Stanton and Freemasonry Lincoln Herald Vol. 95, No. 4 1993 p. 124 – 126

Beauregard, E., The Chief Prosecutor of Andrew Johnson Midwest Quarterly Vol. 31, No. 4 1990 pp. 408 - 422

ben-Jochannon, Y., Black Man of the Nile and His Family African Heritage 1972

Blum, J., The European World: A History Little, Brown & Co. 1966

Boller, P., George Washington and Religion S.M.U. Press 1963

Brodie, F., Thomas Jefferson: An Intimate History Norton 1974

Budge, E.A., A History of Egypt Anthropological Pub. 1968

Bullock, S., Revolutionary Brotherhood: Freemasonry and the Transformation of the American Social Order 1730 – 1840 Univ. of North Carolina 1996

Bullough, V., Homosexuality: A History Garland Press 1979

Bunson, M., A Dictionary of Ancient Egypt Oxford Univ. 1995

Burn, A., & Selincourt, A., Herodotus the Histories Penguin 1972

Buxbaum, M., Critical Essays on Benjamin Franklin Hall 1987

Caffrey, K., The Mayflower Stein & Day 1974

Callahan, C., Washington the Man and the Mason Gibson Bros. 1913

Cantor, N., The Civilization of the Middle Ages Harper Collins 1993

Carruth, G., Encyclopedia of American Facts and Dates Crowell 1956, 1972

Casson, L., Daily Life in Ancient Egypt Time 1972

Cavendish, M., Man, Myth & Magic B.P.C. Publ. 1970 - 1995

Bibliography

Coil, H., Comprehensive View of Freemasonry Macoy Publ. 1973

Coleman J., The Conspirators' Hierarchy: The Committee of 300 Joseph Publ. 1992

Crow, W., History of Magic, Witchcraft and Occultism Wilshire Books 1970

David, R., The Egyptian Kingdoms Elsevier & Phaidon 1975

Davis, C., Western Awakening Appleton, Century, Crofts 1967

De Gregorio, W., Complete Book of U.S. Presidents Dembner 1989

De Lubicz, R., Sacred Science: The King of Pharaonic Theocracy Inner Traditions International 1961

Demott, B., Freemasonry in American Culture and Society Univ. of America 1986

Donald, D., Lincoln Simon & Schuster 1995

Douglas, C., Forty Thousand Quotations July & Co. 1914

Douglass, J., New 20th-Century Encyclopedia of Religious Knowledge Baker 1991

Eigen, L., & Siegel, J., The Macmillan Dictionary of Political Quotations Macmillan Publ. 1993

Fletcher, R., Moorish Spain Holt & Co. 1992

Flexner, J., George Washington and the New Nation Little Brown & Co. 1969

Fresia, J., Toward an American Revolution South End Press 1988

Gardiner, A., Egypt of the Pharaohs Oxford Press 1971

Gay, P., Voltaire: Philosophical Dictionary Basic Books 1962

Goetz, H., Life in the Middle Ages: from the 7th to the 13th century Beck 1986

Goodman, F., Magic Symbols Trodd Publ. House 1989

Greider, W. Secrets of the Temple: How the Federal Reserve Runs the Country Simon & Schuster Inc. 1989

Grimshaw, W., Official History of Freemasonry Among Colored People in North America Broadway 1903

Hall, A., Strange Cults Aldus Books 1976

Hall, M., AN ENCYCLOPEDIC OUTLINE OF Masonic, Hermetic, Qabbalistic and Rosicrucian Symbolical Philosophy The Philosophical Research Soc. 1988

Hall, M., Masonic Orders of Fraternity The Philosophical Research Soc. 1976

Hall, M., The Secret Teachings of All Ages The Philosophical Research Soc. 1977

Handlin, O., Daniel Webster and the Rise of Conservatism Little, Brown & Co. 1955

Higgins, G., Anacalypsis University Books 1965

Hoffer, P., Law and People in Colonial America John Hopkins 1992

Hoyt, R., Life and Thought in the Middle Ages Lund Press 1967

Huart, C., A History of Arabic Literature Khayats 1966

Hudson, H., The Story of the Renaissance Cassell 1912

James, G., Stolen Legacy Philosophical Library 1954

James, M., Andrew Jackson: Portrait of A President Grosset & Dunlap 1937

Jameson, W., Return of Assassin John Wilkes Booth Republic of Texas 1999

Janssen, R. & J., Growing Up in Ancient Egypt Rubicon Press 1990

Jay, T., Encyclopedia of Fads and Fallacies Elliot Right Way Books MCMLVIII

Jeal, T., Livingstone Jeal 1973

Johnson, R., Religious Right Lie: America is a Christian Nation The World Union of Deist http://www.deism.com/think.htm 2000

Jones, R., George Washington Twayne Publ. 1979

Kahaner, L., Cults That Kill Warner Bros. 1988

Kelly, C., Conspiracy Against God and Man Western Islands 1974

Ketcham, R., James Madison: A Biography Macmillan 1971

Kick, R., (ed.), YOU ARE BEING LIED TO: The Disinformation Guide to Media, Historical Whitewashes and Cultural Myths The Disinformation Company LTD 2001

Koch, A., Philosophy of Thomas Jefferson Columbia Univ. 1943

Kohn, G., Encyclopedia of American Scandal Facts on File 1989

Lafeber, W., John Quincy Adams and the American Continental Empire Quadangle Books 1965

Leadbeater, C., The Hidden Life in Freemasonry Theosophical Publ. 1926

Bibliography

Levi, E., & Waite, A. Tr., Dogma Et Rituel de la Haute Magie Rider & Co. 1896 (net ed.) http://www.hermetics.org/pdf/DogmaEtRituel_Part_I.pdf 2001

Lewy, G., The Church and Nazi Germany McGraw-Hill 1964

Lindberg, R., & Number, R., God & Nature Univ. of California 1986

Lipson, D., Freemasonry in Federalist Connecticut 1789 - 1835 Princeton Univ. Press 1977

Lyon, V., Domestic Surveillance: The History of Operation CHAOS Covert Action Information Bulletin ISS. 34 Summer 1990

Martin, E., The Trial of the Templars A.M.S. Press 1978

Melton, J., Encyclopedic Handbook of Cults in America Garland Publ. 1986

Melton, J., Magic, Witchcraft and Paganism in America Garland Publ. 1982

Milele, N., The Journey of the Songhai People Pan African Fed. 1987

Mills, C., The Power Elite Oxford Press 1956

Montet, P., Lives of the Pharaohs World Publ. 1968

Morey, R., The Truth About Masons Harvest House 1993

Morgan, W., Illustrations of Masonry, BY ONE OF THE FRATURNITY, WHO HAS DEVOTED THIRTY YEARS TO THE SUBJECT Gardiner 1826

Morris, R., Seven Who Shaped Our Destiny Fitzhenry & Whiteside 1973

Morse, S., Freemasonry in the American Revolution Masonic Serv. Assn. 1924

Murphy, E., Diodorus on Egypt McFarland 1985

Notestein, W., The English People on the Eve of Colonization 1603 - 1630 Harper & Row 1954

Ovason, D., The Secret Architecture of Our Nation's Capital: The Masons and the Building of Washington D.C. Harper Collins 1999

Paine, T., Of the Religion of Deism Compared with the Christian Religion The World Union of Deist http://www.deism.com/paine_essay01.htm 8-20-02

Peabody, J., The Founding Fathers: John Adams A Biography in His own Words Harper & Row 1973

Percival, H., Masonry and its Symbols The Word Foundation 1988

The Founders' Facade

Peterson, M., Thomas Jefferson & The New Nation: A Biography Oxford Univ. 1970

Pfeifer, C., The Dead Sea Scrolls and the Bible Weathervein 1969

Pike, A., Morals and Dogma of the Ancient and Accepted Scottish Rite of Freemasonry Charleston A∴M∴ 5641

Platt, S., Respectfully Quoted Library of Congress 1989

Preuss, A., Dictionary of Secret and Other Societies Herder Publ. 1924

Quarles, B., The Negro in the American Revolution Univ. of North Carolina Press 1961

Ragsdale, L., Vital Statistics of the Presidency: Washington to Clinton Congressional Quarterly 1996

Randolph, P., Hermes Mercurius Trigismestus: his Divine Pymander Randolph 1871 - 1889

Richards, L., The Life and Times of Congressman John Quincy Adams Oxford Univ. Press 1986

Robertson, J., Short History of Freethought Russell & Russell 1957

Robinson, J., Proofs of a Conspiracy Western Islands 1967

Rogers, J.A., Sex and Race Rogers Publ. 1967

Roper, H., Hitler's Secret Conversations 1941 - 1944 Octagon Books 1972

Ropes, L., Aristotle Black Inc. 1943

Rosen, R., A Short History of Charleston Lexikos 1982

Roth, P., Masonry in the Formation of Our Government 1761 – 1799 Atlas 1927

Rousseau, J., On the Social Contract Hackett Publ. 1987

Rousseau, J., The Social Contract Penguin 1968

Schmidt, A., Fraternal Organizations Greenwood Press 1980

Schwartz, B., George Washington: The Making of an American Symbol The Free Press 1987

Schwartz, T., & Empey, D., Satanism: Is Your Family Safe Zondervan 1988

Schlesinger, A., The Age of Jackson Little, Brown & Co. 1953

Schleshinger, A., The History of American Presidential Elections 1789 - 1968 Chelsea House 1985

Seldes, G., One Thousand Americans Boni & Gaer 1947

Bibliography

Seldes, G., The Great Quotations Pocket Books 1960, 1967

Simons, G., Barbarian Europe Timelife 1968

Smith, B., Bradford of Plymouth Lippincott 1951

Spivak, J., A Man in His Time Horizon Press 1967

Tatch, J., Freemasonry in the Thirteen Colonies MaCoy 1929

Tompkins, P., The Magic of Obelisks Harper & Row 1981

Turner, W., Rearview Mirror: looking back at the F.B.I., C.I.A., and other tails Penmarin Books 2001

Uphill, E., Egyptian Towns and Cities Shire Publ. 1988

Vaughn, W., The Anti-Masonic Party in the United States 1826 - 1848 Univ. of Kentucky Press 1982

Wallace, P., The White Roots of Peace Univ. of Penn. 1946

Wallenchinsky, D., & Wallace, I., The Peoples Almanac II Wm Morrow 1978

Walters, K., Rational Infidels: The American Deists Longwood 1992

Walters, K., The American Deist: Voices of Reason and Dissent in the Early Republic Univ. of Kansas 1992

Whalen, W., Christianity and American Freemasonry Ignatius Press 1998

Woods, R., The World Treasury of Religious Quotations Hawthorn Books 1966

_____., 200 Years: A Bicentennial Illustrated History of the United States Books by U.S. News and World Report

_____., Albert Pike, Mystic Pt 1 http://www.mastermason.com/lodge850/Reading/pikemystic1.htm 5-2-4

_____., American Freemasonry: A Delusional Cultural Foundation for Repressive Social Control http://www.crocker.com/~acacia/text_mabook.html 4-1-98

_____., Astrology: Dragons throughout the ages - Dragons importance in Astrology The Experience Enterprise http://www.experiencefestival.com/index.php/topic/articles/article/1106 04-23-04

The Founders' Facade

_____., Bill Moyers Address: Inequality Matters – June 3, 2004 N.Y.C. http://inequality.org/moyerstranscript.pdf

_____., Book TV: In Depth – Gore Vidal (Video) C-Span 10/1/00

_____., Booknotes: Kenneth Davis Interview: Don't Know Much About History (Video) C-Span 9/91

_____., Books on Freemasonry: Antimasonic books & pamphlets from the 19th and early 20th century http://www.crocker.com/~acacia/antim.html 4-1-98

_____, By George What a City! http://masons.gntech.net/byGeorgeWhataCity.htm 2004

_____., Chronicle of America Chronicle Publ 1989

_____., Collier's Encyclopedia Macmillan 1986

_____., Congressional Quarterly Guide to U.S. Elections Congressional Quarterly Inc. 1994

_____., CounterPunch – CNN AND PSYOPS http://www.counterpunch.org/cnnpsyops.html 07-23-02

_____., Dictionary of American Biography Scribner's Sons 1936

_____., Dictionary of American History Charles Scribner's Sons 1976

_____., Did You Know? Under the pressure of war, the Corps built the Pentagon in 16 months? U.S. Corps of Army Engineers http://www.hq.usace.army.mil/history/vignettes/vignette_34.htm 04-23-04

_____., Encyclopaedia Judaica Macmillan 1971

_____., Encyclopedia Americana Grolier Publ. 2001

_____., Encyclopedia of Philosophy Macmillan Freepress 1973

_____., Encyclopedia of Religion Macmillan 1987

_____., Esso pictorial guide to Washington, D.C., and vicinity : 1942 (net)

_____., Famous Freemasons http://www.masonicinfo.com/famous.htm 4-24-04

_____., Famous Masons http://www.mn-mason.org/famous.html 4-1-98

_____., Freemasonry and Washington D.C.'s Street Layout http://www.freemasonrywatch.org/washington.html 2-2-2004

Bibliography

_____., Freemasonry Source Confirms our Article: Masonic Symbols of Power in Their Seat of Power http://www.cuttingedge.org/n1081.html 7-28-98

_____., Freemasonry Watch: KGB – It was Johnson http://freemasonrywatch.org/LATimes.html 5-2-04

_____., Freemasonry Watch: Monitoring the World's Largest Secret Society http://www.freemasonrywatch.org/index.html 5-2-4

_____., Freemasonry Watch: The Crown and the Capitol – Abraham Lincoln http://freemasonrywatch.org/lincoln.html 5-2 -4 & http://speciesofangel.serverpro2.com/featured//zero12.htm 07-15-02

_____., Freemasonry Watch: The Crown and the Capitol – It was Johnson http://www.freemasonrywatch.org/lincoln.html 5-2-4 & http://speciesofangel.serverpro2.com/featured//zero12.htm 07-23-02

_____., Freemasonry Watch: The First Degree of Freemasonry Watch http://freemasonrywatch.org/1index.html 5 -2 4

_____., Freemasons http://www.freedomdomain.com/freemason.html 07-14-02

_____., Friend To Friend http://www.aracnet.com/-mult1/pageone.shtml 8-9-99

_____., Frontline: The Secret File on J. Edgar Hoover (Video) P.B.S. 1993

_____., Grolier Multimedia Encyclopedia Grolier 1997

_____., Gypsies: Wanderers of the World National Geographic 1970

_____., Historical Statistics of the United States: Colonial Times to 1957 U.S. Dept. of Commerce 1961

_____., Historical Statistics of the United States: Colonial Times to 1970 pt. I, U.S. Dept. of Commerce 1975

_____., History's Mysteries: The Plot to Overthrow F.D.R. (Video) Weller-Grossman 1999

_____., History's Mysteries: Witchcraft (Video) History Channel 10-27-01

_____., Inside the Third Reich: Memoir by Albert Speer Macmillan 1970

_____., Jefferson Library of America 1984

The Founders' Facade

_____., Lawmakers blast Pledge ruling CNN.Com/Lawcenter http://www.cnn.com/2002/LAW/06/26/pledge.allegiance/index.html 06-27-02

_____., List of Famous Freemasons http://www.balaams-ass.com/journal/warnings/masnfame.htm 4-2-98

_____., Political Parties and Elections in the United States Garland Publ. 1991

_____., Ron's Currency, Stocks & Bonds: The History of U.S. Paper Money http://www.ronscurrency.com/rhist.htm 5-20-04

_____., Teaching Politics: Images of American Political History http://teachpol.tcnj.edu/ 7-23-04 - (*Images on page viii, 25, 36, 38, and 93 are courtesy of this website and Dr. William J. Ball.*)

_____., Templar History: Eliphas Lévi - The Man Behind Baphomet http://www.templarhistory.com/levi.html 5-2-4

_____., The Address of the National Anti-Masonic Convention to the People of the United States 9-11-1830

_____., The American Peoples Encyclopedia Spencer Press 1955

_____., The Encyclopedia Britannica Encyclopedia Britannica 1973 - 1995

_____., The Encyclopedia of Discovery and Exploration Doubleday 1971

_____., The Freemasons: institutionalised parasites? http://www.tlio.demon.co.uk/masons.htm 4-2-98

_____., The Greenwood Encyclopedia of American Institutions, Political Parties and Civil Action Groups Greenwood Press 1981

_____., The KKK and the KOL, "Masonic" brotherhoods which suppressed reforms http://users.crocker.com/~acacia/kol_cult.html 08-27-02

_____., The Kybalion: Hermetic Philosophy Yoga 1912

_____., The National Cyclopedia of American Biography White & Co. 1898 (onward)

_____., The Papers of George Washington http://gwpapers.virginia.edu/presidency/electoral.html 07-20-02

Bibliography

_____., The Philosophical Research Society: Freemasonry http://www.prs.org/book059.htm 7-13-98

_____., The Plot to Seize the White House (review by Dale Wharton) http://www.eclectica.org/v1n1/reviews/wharton/_plot.html 8-6-99

_____., The Riddle of the Dead Sea Scrolls (Video) Discovery Chan. Mitchell 1990

_____., The Scottish Rite Journal http://www.srmason-sj.org/council/journal/feb98/TRESFEB.HTM 7-13-98

_____., The Western Tradition: The Middle Ages (Video) Annenburg 1989

_____., The World Book Encyclopedia World Book Inc. 1970 - 2003

_____., The World of Joseph Campbell: The Story of Parzival (Video) William Free 1989

_____., The World of the Native American National Geographic 1974

_____., The World's Greatest Conspiracies (Video) Arts & Entertainment 1997

_____., The Writings of Henry D. Thoreau http://www.library.ucsb.edu/depts/thoreau/bfaq.html 11-29-98

_____., Transformation of a Myth through Time: Campbell Lecture Series (Video) W. Free 1989

_____., UK: The Craft BBC Online Network http://news2.thisbbc.co.uk/hi/english/uk/newsid%5f353000/353412.stm 5-26-99

_____., Universal Standard Encyclopedia W. Funk 1955

_____., World Almanac and Book of Facts 2002 World Almanac Books 2002

_____., World: Europe freemason report urges more openness BBC Online Network http://news2.thls.bbc.co.uk/hi/english/world/europe/newsid%5F352000/352966.stm 5-26-99

_____., Writings: Franklin Library of America 1987

Index

A

Abercrombie, J., 16
Adams, J., 16, 18
Adams, J.Q., 16, 18, 32, 71, 92, 93
Adonai 80
Allen, E., 13, 15
Alviella, G., 44
American Legion 82
American Liberty League 82
Ancients 56, 57, 62
Anderson, J., 49
Anti-Masonic Convention 63, 64, 69, 71, 72, 74
Anti-Masonic Enquirer 71
Anti-Masonic Party 71, 72, 73, 74, 75, 77
Arabia 48
Arcesilaus, Plan of 55
Arnold, B., 58
Aristotle v, 1, 19, 33, 35, 36, 40
Articles of Confederation 30
Aryan 78, 79
Asian Immigrants 33
Aurelius, M., iv
Australia 5

B

Babylon 63
Bacon, F., 4
Baphomet 46, 71, 73, 78, 80, 81, 89, 90, 94, 95
Baptists 8
Barton, W., 95
Barvaria 55
Beecher, L., 22
Bel 80
Bill of Rights 11, 28
Black Codes 33
Black Soldiers 28
Blake, W., 14
Blavatsky, M., 94
Blount, C., 12
Blount, W., 18
Booth, J., 77
Bradford, W., 7
Brahma 78
Bruce, E., 66, 70
Bruno, G., 12
Buddha (Bouddh) 79
Burke, A., 62
Butler, p., 18
Butler, S., 82, 83,

C

C.I.A. 55, 62, 75
CNN 55
Calvinism 7, 8, 13
Campbell, J., 47, 94
Canada 5, 57, 58, 78
Capitol 88, 89, 90, 93
Carnegie, A., 76

Carr, P., 18
Cassius 60, 61, 62
Cayugas 31
Charles I 44
Charles II 50
Cheseboro, N., 64, 65
Chief Deganawidah 31
Christ 15, 16, 17, 18, 21, 23, 24, 25, 47
Chubb, T., 12
Church of England 6, 7, 8, 9, 24
Cicero 21
Cincinnati, 60, 61, 62, 88
Civil War 77
Clay, H., 74
Clement 7
Clement V 46
Cockburn, A., 55
Coleman, J., 75
Collins, A., 12
Cologne 43
Committee on Un-American Activities 82, 83
Connecticut 8, 72
Constant, A., 78, 95
Constitution ii, 15, 23, 24, 25, 28, 29, 30, 32, 33, 34, 57, 58, 84
Cox, D., 56, 58,
Crata Repoa 41
Cromwell, O., 7, 45
Crusades 45

Index

D

D'Alembert 22
Dartmouth 22, 23
David 85, 95
Davis, J., 63
de Vries, A., 55
Declaration of Independence 11, 18, 57, 58
Deistical Soc. 13
Desaguliers, J., 52, 53
Devil (see Baphomet)
Diogenes 22
Dragon's Head 88, 89, 95
Druids 48
Dutch 2, 3, 53, 55
Dyer, R., 63

E

E Pluribus Unum 85, 87
Egypt 40, 41, 42, 48, 52, 95
Eiffel Tower 91
Einstein, A., 83, 97
Electoral College 32, 74
Elizabeth, Queen., 3, 44
Ellmaker, A., 73
Ellsworth, O., 18
Esquire 27

F

Feudalism 59
Filmore, M., 71
Forrest, N., 78
Fort Niagara 65, 67
Fourth Psychological Operations Group 55
France 2, 3, 5, 9, 40, 43, 45, 46, 50, 53, 55, 57, 58, 61, 78, 91
Franklin, B., 13, 17, 18, 21, 25, 30, 53, 58, 61, 70, 95
Frederick, Prince of Wales 53

G

Gandhi iv
Geometry 87
George, H., 76
George II 4
Georgia 4, 9, 33, 55
Germany 9, 55
Grandfather Clause 33
Grant, U., 25

H

Hakluyt, R., 3, 4
Hamilton, A., 11, 15, 25, 28, 29, 35
Har-oeri (Horus) 82, 95
Harrison, w., 74
Harvard 23

Hermes 87
Higgins, G., 49, 50
Hitler, A., 20, 40
Herbert, Lord 12
Hobbes, T., 12
Holocaust 40
Hoover, J., 79
Hopkins, H., 70
House of Representatives 31, 32
House of the Temple 79, 90, 91
Hume, D., 12
Hungary 55

I

Illumnati 54, 55, 60, 75
Ireland 56
Iroquois 3, 31, 32
Isis 82
Italy 43, 46, 50, 55
Ivins, M., 76

J

Jackson, A., 18, 25, 32, 38, 73, 74, 75
James I 4, 44
James II 50, 51, 58
Japan 20
Jay, J., 29, 34
Jefferson, T., 11, 13, 14, 15, 18, 23, 24, 25, 28, 70

Johnson, A., 77, 78
Johnson, L., 77

K

Kant, I., 12
Kennedy, J., 77, 92, 93, 97
Khaldun, I., 20
Know Nothings 75, 77
Krishna 78
Ku Klux Klan 33, 78

L

L' Enfant, P., 88
Lawson, L., 66
Lessing, G., 12
Lincoln, A., 25, 32, 34, 76, 77, 78
Livingstone, D., 4
Livy 18
Lloyd, H., 76
Locke, J., 11, 20
Louisiana, 5, 77
Lucifer (see Baphomet)

M

MacArthur, D., 83
Machiavelli 21
Mackey, A., 77
MacNider, H., 83

Madison, J., 13, 15, 18, 23, 29, 34
Magna Carta 31
Mann, T., iv
Manous 79
Marten, H., 12
Martin, L., 18
Marshall, T., 33, 34
Mason, G., 18
Massachusetts 6, 8, 9, 34, 72, 78, 79, 92
Massasoit 6
Masonic Congress 45, 47
Masonic Triangle 78, 84
Mayflower 5
McClure, D., 14, 16
McCormick-Dickstein Committee 82
Mercer, J., 18
Miller, D., 63
Mithras 80
Moderns 56, 57
Moloch 80
Monch, G., 45
Monroe, J., 13, 18
Montesquieu, C., 11
Morgan, W., 50, 63, 64, 65, 66, 67, 68, 69, 70, 73, 74, 87, 88
Morgan, T., 12
Moses 16
Mohawks 31

N

Native Americans 3, 5, 6, 18, 31, 33, 37, 38, 58
Natural Religion 10, 11
New Deal 82
New Hampshire 9
New Jersey 9
New York 58, 64, 67, 71, 72, 73, 74
Newton, I., 48, 49, 52, 59
Nietzsche, F., iv, 79
Nonconformists 7
North Carolina 9, 55

O

Oglethorpe, J., 4
Olympians 75
Oneidas 30
Onondagas 31
Osiris 52, 80, 82
Owen, R., 16

P

Paine, T., 12, 13, 15, 23, 70
Palmer, E., 13
Palmer, J., 52
Pantheon 91
Parzival 47
Paul 7, 79
Pennsylvania 9, 72
Pentagon 89, 95

Index

Philip IV 46
Phoenix 87, 93
Pickney, C., 18
Pickney, C. C., 18
Pike, A., 77, 78, 79, 80, 81, 82, 90, 91, 95
Pilgrims 5, 6, 7
Pledge of Allegiance 25, 30
Plymouth Rock 5, 6, 7
Polybius 19
Portugal 40, 46
Presidency 31, 32
Price, H., 61
Prince Hall, 79
Princeton 22
Principia 53

Q

Quakers 8, 9
Quartering Act 28

R

Ra 91
Raleigh, W., 3
Randolph, E., 19
Regulators of North Carolina 34
Reimarus, H., 12
Reincarnation 48
Rhodesia 5
Roosevelt, F., 82

Rosicrucians 47, 48
Rousseau, J., 11, 12, 20, 22
Ru 94
Rush, B., 23, 28
Russia 50, 55
Rutledge, J., 19

S

Sackville, T., 44
Samoset 6
Samuel, W., 18
Satan (see Baphomet)
Sawyer, E., 66
Scotland   41, 49, 53, 77, 84
Senate 31
Seneca iv, 19
Senecas 31
Seward, W., 71
Shay's Rebellion 34
Shelton, J., 66
Shiva (Siva) 78, 94
Siculus, D., 19
Sirius 95
Skull and Bones 75
Slavery 6, 18, 20, 27
Smallpox 37
Solomon 42, 85, 95
Somervell, B., 89
South Carolina 9, 62
Spain 2, 3, 40, 46
Spinoza, B., 12
Squanto 6

Stamp Act 27
Stanton, E., 77
Stearns, J., 62, 63
Steuben, F., 60, 61
Stevens, T., 71
Stiles, E., 17
Strasbourg 43
Sugar Act 27
Sweden 2, 55
Switzerland 50

T

Tacitus 18
Tarot 94
Templars 45, 46, 47, 48, 49, 60
Tennessee 75
Tertullian 20
Thomson, C., 84
Thoreau 23
Thoth 95
Thucydides iv
Tindal, M., 12
Tocqueville, A., 21
Toland, J., 12
Tories 57
Townsend Act 27
Trail of Tears 38
Turner, T., 20
Tuscaroras 31
Tzu, S., 55

U

Unitarianism 16, 18, 19
United States, Currency ("*In God We Trust*") 17, 25
Unites States, Seal 84, 85, 86, 87, 94, 95
United States, Wealth Distribution 36

V

Valance, H., 66, 67, 68, 69
Valley Forge 16
Van Burien, M., 74
Vanini, L., 12
Vedas 78
Vermont 73
Vidal, G., 62
Vienna 43
Viret, P., 13
Virginia 3, 6, 9, 23, 77
Virgo 88, 89, 95
Volney, C., 11
Voltaire, F., 12, 22, 32
von Goethe, J.W., 77
Von Hund, Baron 49, 50

W

Wall Street 35, 82
Washington D.C. 38, 87, 88, 89, 90, 91
Washington, G., 13, 16, 17, 18, 21, 25, 32, 57, 61, 70, 88, 93
Washington Monument 52, 88, 89, 90, 91
Weed, T., 71
Weems 16, 17
Whig Party 74, 75
Whigs 57
White, B., 16
White House 88, 89, 90, 91, 95
William and Mary 18, 22
William of Orange 51
Williard, J., 75
Wilson, B., 16, 18
Wirt, W., 73, 74
Witchcraft 9
Wraxhall, P., 37
Wright, F., 16

Y

Yale 22
Yeshua (see Christ)

Z

Zahed, E., (see Constant, A.,)
Zeus 80
Zurich 43

The Founders' Facade

Order Form

If you would like to purchase a copy (or copies) of The Founders' Façade, feel free to photocopy this page and use the copy as an order form. Just fill in the information and mail the sale price of $19.95 plus $3.00 shipping and handling for each book to the address below (money orders please). For orders of 50 books or more - contact us via email to learn about our volume discounts and/or organization donations.

Name: _____

Address: _____

_____

_____

Phone: _____

Number of Books purchased: _____

Amount enclosed: _____

KornerStone Books
6947 Coal Creek Pkwy
Suite 206
Newcastle, WA 98059
Kornerstone@execs.com

www.ingramcontent.com/pod-product-compliance
Lightning Source LLC
Chambersburg PA
CBHW080251170426
43192CB00014BA/2638